ON DEMAND

for the Common Core State Standards Assessments

Writing
ON DEMAND

for the Common Core State Standards Assessments

Kelly Sassi & Anne Ruggles Gere

with Leila Christenbury

HEINEMANN
Portsmouth, NH

Heinemann
361 Hanover Street
Portsmouth, NH 03801–3912
www.heinemann.com

Offices and agents throughout the world

The authors and publisher wish to thank those who have generously given permission to reprint borrowed material. Every effort has been made to contact the copyright holders for permission to reprint borrowed material where necessary. We regret any oversights that may have occurred and would be happy to rectify them in future printings of this work.

Excerpts from The PARCC Assessment (2012, 2013) from http://parcconline.org. Reprinted by permission of PARCC.

Excerpts from the Common Core State Standards © Copyright 2010. National Governors Association Center for Best Practices and Council of Chief State School Officers. All rights reserved.

Excerpts from the SBAC Assessment (2012, 2013) from www.smarterbalanced.org. Reprinted by permission of Smarter Balanced Assessment Consortium.

Excerpt from "A Revision of Bloom's Taxonomy: An Overview" by David R. Krathwohl from *Theory into Practice* (November 1, 2002, vol. 41, no. 4, pp. 212–218). Reprinted by permission of Taylor & Francis Ltd, http://www.tandf.co.uk/journals.

(Credit lines continue on page vi)

Library of Congress Cataloging-in-Publication Data
Sassi, Kelly, author.
   Writing on demand for the Common Core State Standards assessments / Kelly Sassi, Anne Ruggles Gere, with Leila Christenbury.
      pages cm.
   Includes bibliographical references and index.
   ISBN 978-0-325-05085-0
   1. English language—Composition and exercises—Study and teaching—United States. 2. Education—Standards—United States. I. Gere, Anne Ruggles, author. II. Title.
   LB1576.S26 2014
   372.62'3—dc23   2013043042

Editor: Holly Kim Price
Production: Hilary Goff
Cover design: Suzanne Heiser
Interior design: Monica Ann Crigler
Typesetter: Publishers' Design and Production Services, Inc.
Manufacturing: Steve Bernier

Printed in the United States of America on acid-free paper

18 17 16 15 14   EBM   1 2 3 4 5

*To teachers everywhere who dig deep
into their hearts and minds every day to
help students realize their potential.*

Online Resources

To access this additional material, please visit **www.heinemann.com/writingondemandccssa**.

Contents

Acknowledgments

We are both grateful to the many students and teachers who generously shared their work with us. We really appreciate the graduate students who provided assistance in a variety of ways, from tracking down resources to tagging words for our index. Thank you, Vickie Conner, Steven Hammer, M. K. Laughlin, Cindy Marihart, and Sara Miller. Special thanks to Enrico Sassi for help with Heinemann's format requirements.

Kelly is grateful to the leadership team of the Red River Valley Writing Project: Kim Donehower, Nancy Devine, Pam Fisher, and Jessica Zerr for mentoring and support. The summer institute, writer's workshops, and writing retreat (thank you, Maplelag staff!) gave her the time and space to generate initial ideas about this project. Kelly also thanks the administrators and teachers of West Fargo Public Schools, especially the perceptive and passionate curriculum coordinator, Kathy Scott, whose sharp eye and generous use of the "forward" button put many materials in her in-box. Kathy's support, along with that of Louise Dardis, Molly Bestge, and David Flowers, provided opportunities to work with and learn from dozens of smart secondary teachers in their district. Special thanks to teachers Alissa Helm, Lisa Fricke, and Dan Dooher who shared their work and/or the work of their students with us.

Anne extends her thanks to the many teachers who offer powerful models for meeting the challenges of helping their students become effective writers in an era when test scores threaten to dominate more significant educational goals. In particular, she is grateful to the insights offered by Laura Mahler, Leah Barnett, Julie Martinez, Peter Haun, Katie Lacano, Steve Snead, Linda Denstaedt, and Pete Shaheen. Special thanks to Tasha Rios, Kevin Galvin, Paula Gentile, and Sarah Guzick for sharing their own and their students' work. Anne is also thankful to the entire Sassi family: Anna, Renato, Egle, Paola, Enrico, Alex, Max, and, especially Kelly, for making it such fun to write this book. And, of course, she is eternally grateful to Budge and Denali, who brighten every day.

Kelly thanks her life partner, Enrico Sassi, her sons, Alessandro and Massimo, and all her Italian in-laws for their interest in the work and tireless support. We will always think fondly of the staff at Le Graal Café in Montgenevre, France, which became our temporary "office" in summer 2013.

Both Anne and Kelly are sorry that Leila Christenbury was unable to co-author this book, but, as the title page indicates, her wise and inspiring views of teaching are present on its pages.

Last, but not least, Kelly and Anne thank their editor, Holly Kim Price, for her support of this project and Hilary Goff for seeing it through to the end.

Chapter One

Unpacking the Common Core
State Standards in Writing

CHAPTER OVERVIEW *This chapter provides strategies for:*

- *meeting Common Core State Standards in reading, writing, speaking, and listening*

- *unpacking and analyzing the Common Core State Standards that should be undertaken collaboratively across disciplines and grade levels*

- *analyzing the Common Core State Standards and understanding how doing so leads to shifts in pedagogy*

- *thinking through how writing on demand and reading on demand are necessary skills to complete the performance assessments aligned with the Common Core State Standards*

- *developing writers who can confidently contend with a multitude of writing situations.*

Introduction

The Common Core State Standards (CCSS) are a new phenomenon in the United States. For the first time, most states have signed on to adopt standards that are common among states. Although this move is problematic given that all states already had standards that many professionals had worked hard on, and the National Council of Teachers of English has an excellent set of standards created through a rigorous, collaborative process, the CCSS offer uniformity so that a student moving from Maine to Colorado, for example, will encounter similar educational standards and assessment.

Still, this change is frightening when we consider the possible implications and the unknowns. For individual educators, who are often doing heroic jobs in challenging conditions, the unknowns can seem overwhelming. For many teachers, the first reaction to Common Core was denial, quickly followed by anger. We—Anne and Kelly—have been on the ground working with teachers as they move through these emotions. By now, most seem to be emerging from the lowest point, largely thanks to an unexpected consequence of teaching in the era of Common Core standards: the emergence of new conversations about teaching writing.

Teachers are now collaborating across grade levels, across the K–12/higher education divide, across content areas, and across states. This is a good thing, too—no teacher should have to negotiate this new landscape alone. Teachers in California, in Indiana, and in New York are all making similar shifts, and this book brings some of their voices together.

About This Book

The Common Core State Standards in writing are for every content area teacher to use. With this in mind, we have written this book not only for teachers of English Language Arts, but for all teachers who, working together, can make a tremendously positive impact on the writing abilities of American students. With this diverse audience in mind, we have created particular features that are found in each chapter of this book.

PLC Activities. In each chapter we include activities for Professional Learning Communities (PLCs) whose members may be working together to deal with the Common Core State Standards and Assessments. These activities help teachers dig deeper into the ideas in this book and try out new practices before taking them to the classroom.

Notes on College Readiness. To build a bridge between secondary teachers and college teachers, we include concepts from the "Framework for Success in Postsecondary Writing," a publication of the National Council of Teachers of English, the Council of Writing Program Administrators, and the National Writing Project. This document describes what college readiness looks like from the perspective of college-level instructors. We also provide some context and history that will help answer some important questions: How did we get here? Why do we do things this way? How is this similar to or different from what has come before?

Classroom Moves. This section includes lessons and activities that, along with variations for different content areas, teachers can use in the classroom. We demonstrate the specific kinds of writing activities that will help students meet the challenge of writing on demand.

Research and Political Considerations. Let's face it: Teaching in the era of CCSS is highly political. Many important standards, best practices, and true college-ready activities are either not explicitly mentioned in the Common Core Standards or missing altogether. This section includes links to NCTE Policy Research Briefs, Position Statements, and other professional documents that will help teachers make the argument for good curricular decisions. These documents are designed to bring research into political discussions. In this chapter, we include a research brief on standards implementation.

Guiding Principles of This Book

This book proceeds from six classroom-tested assumptions.

Changes in Assessment Help Shape Instruction

Students should learn how to use assessment (including the forms represented by writing on demand) to improve their own writing. By becoming effective evaluators of their own and others' writing, students will improve as writers and, at the same time, perform better in contexts that ask them to write on demand. Similarly, when we understand what the new assessments do (and don't) tell us about our students' writing skills, we can adjust instruction to make sure our students are truly "college and career ready," not just ready for a high-stakes test.

Writing Prompts Employ Rhetorically Shaped Language

Whether one considers an assignment given in a composition class or a prompt on a CCSS-mandated test, the language used to tell students what and how to write provides rhetorical cues. Students can learn how to read writing prompts more effectively if they have a basic understanding of the principles of rhetoric. Teaching rhetorical skills not only helps students contend with writing on demand tasks, but it also contributes to "writing transfer" (Clark 2012). Writing transfer is the ability to take writing skills learned in one context (such as English class) and apply them to another context (such as science class or the work world). We believe in broadening students' experiences with rhetorical situations.

Writing Skills Should Be Developed by Content Area Teachers as well as Language Arts Teachers

The strategies for successful writing on demand apply to content area teachers, too. Citing the Alliance for Excellent Education's "Literacy Instruction in the Content Areas": "Content areas literacy must be a cornerstone of any movement to build high-quality secondary schools." This view is reinforced by the CCSS's focus on literacy standards for social studies/history, science, and technical subjects.

A Vertical Approach Fosters Writing Improvement

Writing is not learned quickly or once for all time. It is learned best over an extended time period, and that learning is frequently recursive. Accordingly, the best writing instruction takes a vertical approach, with one class building on another, and the CCSS affirm this model. This scaffolding of concepts from one grade level to another is particularly helpful in preparing students for writing on demand because it fosters confidence and familiarity with many forms of writing. Citing the National Commission on Writing once again, "standards, curriculum, and assessment must be aligned, in writing and elsewhere in the curriculum, in reality as well as in rhetoric" (4).

Text-Dependent Writing Requires Focused Instruction

Although the CCSS have separate reading and writing standards, they emphasize the integration of the two, and this book fosters that integration by helping students focus on the details of prose. Attention to how phrases, sentences, and paragraphs are put together will give students a broader repertoire to draw upon in their own writing, especially when they compose under the pressure of a timed test. Furthermore, the new CCSS assessments differ from previous writing-on-demand tests (ACT, SAT, and AP, for example) in that they often require students to read an informational text or view a video and then use textual evidence to support their stance in an essay. The ability to read complex texts in a limited amount of time and respond to the text in writing is new, and it requires different pedagogy for teachers who have not emphasized this skill in the past.

Criteria for Evaluation Belong in the Classroom

Since we wrote our first book on this topic, *Writing on Demand: Best Practices and Strategies for Success*, there is more widespread use of rubrics, and today's students have a better idea of how their writing will be evaluated. New research shows that students can improve their own writing when they develop a better understanding of what readers expect. Furthermore, when teachers and students examine evaluative criteria together, the distance between classroom and large-scale assessment is decreased. This book will provide details of both the PARCC (Partnership for Assessment of Readiness for College and Careers) and Smarter Balanced Assessment Consortium (SBAC) approaches to writing assessment as well as guidance on how to help students understand this new kind of writing evaluation. However, we will also talk about ways to help students become more independent in the way they seek out standards for writing and, hopefully, even internalize their own standards. This is because much of the writing they will do as adults will not come with a rubric. Have you ever had a boss ask you to compose a report and then give you a rubric outlining her or his expectations? Students will eventually have to use their own judgment when revising and evaluating their writing.

Notes on College Readiness: *College Readiness in History*

The CCSS focus on preparing students to be college ready might suggest that this is a new concern for schools and teachers, but the history of preparing students for college and assessing their level of accomplishment extends back to the late nineteenth century. In 1894 the National Conference on Uniform Entrance Requirements in English endorsed the recommendations of the Committee of Ten for annual Uniform Lists of books on which college applicants would write essays. These essays would determine which students were accepted at a specific college.

The lists were divided into two types: a list of five or six books on which the college examinations would be based, and a longer list of texts for more general study. Implicit in the work of the National Conference and the Committee of Ten was the assumption that the goal of high school is to prepare students for college.

Not surprisingly, the Uniform Lists had a powerful effect on the high school curriculum, and some of the texts included on these lists—Shakespeare's *Julius Caesar* and *Merchant of Venice*, Sir Walter Scott's *Ivanhoe*, Charles Dickens' *A Tale of Two Cities*, Henry David Thoreau's *Walden*, Nathaniel Hawthorne's *House of Seven Gables*, and George Eliot's *Silas Marner*—remained in high school book depositories long after the Uniform Lists had been replaced by the College Board's SAT exam.

Now, as when the National Conference attempted to standardize college entrance requirements, national groups have an interest in assuring the public that students are college ready. It may be worth considering, however, the composition of these groups. The Committee of Ten was comprised of college presidents and two heads of private high schools, and the members of the National Conference were all educators. The Common Core State Standards were called into being by the National Governor's Association and the Council of Chief State School Officers.

Getting Ready to Unpack the Standards: Surveying the Shifts

The Common Core is focused on creating young adults who are "college and career ready." But what does this mean, really? It is worthwhile to analyze the standards and understand the key changes they bring to teaching and learning, as well as to think about whether they serve larger goals of our education system.

By now, most agree that the CCSS assessments will require some global shifts in how teachers approach writing instruction. Writing on demand is one of those shifts. Common Core Standard #10 explicitly targets writing on demand as well as process writing: "Write routinely over extended time frames (time for research, reflection, and revision) and shorter time frames (*a single sitting* or a day or two) for a range of tasks, purposes, and audiences" (emphasis added). According to PARCC, one of the two testing consortia, the common core shifts have to do with knowledge, text complexity, and the use of evidence from text. *EngageNY*, a website created by the New York Education Department, also describes some shifts, but includes more detail. The shifts are compared in Figure 1.1.

Figure 1.1 Pedagogical Shifts Demanded by Common Core State Standards

Online 1.1
Pedagogical Shifts Demanded by Common Core State Standards

According to PARCC	According to *EngageNY*		
Knowledge: The standards require building knowledge through content-rich nonfiction.	Shift 1	Balancing informational and literary texts	Students read a true balance of informational and literary texts.
	Shift 2	Knowledge in the disciplines	Students build knowledge about the world (domains/content areas) through TEXT rather than the teacher or activities.
Complexity: The standards require regular practice with complex text and its academic language.	Shift 3	Staircase of complexity	Students read the central, grade-appropriate text around which instruction is centered. Teachers are patient; they create more time, space, and support in the curriculum for close reading.
Evidence: The standards emphasize reading and writing grounded in evidence from text, both literary and informational.	Shift 4	Text-based answers	Students engage in rich and rigorous evidence-based conversations about text.
	Shift 5	Writing from sources	Writing emphasizes use of evidence from sources to inform or make an argument.
	Shift 6	Academic vocabulary	Students constantly build the transferable vocabulary they need to access grade-level complex texts. This can be done effectively by spiraling like content in increasingly complex texts.

(Partnership for Assessment of Readiness for College and Careers. PARCC Online. http://www.parcconline.org/samples/item-task-prototypes)

(From EngageNY.org of the New York State Education Department. "Common Core Shifts." Internet. Available from www.engageny.org/resource/common-core-shifts; accessed 7 February 2014.)

PLC ACTIVITY

In your professional learning community (PLC), department, team, school, or district committee, try this activity to explore how all teachers in the group view the shifts in the teaching of writing.

1. List the kinds of writing your students currently do in your class.

2. Compare the kinds of writing you currently do with the kinds of writing emphasized in Figure 1.1.

3. Share as a group—have one person tabulate the results from the individuals.

4. Ask the group: What kinds of literacy needs are we successfully meeting? Is there any kind of literacy we should be spending more time on? For example, should students be reading more informational texts? If so, which course(s) can meet this need?

5. Follow up: Bring samples from various content area courses, analyze the level of text complexity as a group, and then discuss ways to help students read these texts. We discuss how to analyze the level of complexity of a text in Chapter 2.

Unpacking the Standards

The Common Core State Standards are divided into four strands: reading, writing, speaking/listening, and language. For the purpose of this book, we will focus primarily on reading, writing, and language, because these strands are the dominant ones in writing on demand for common core performance assessments. However, we believe that a literacy-rich environment that includes substantive speaking and listening activities also contributes to students' development as writers. Analysis of the standards is best done in the company of colleagues. Some teachers started unpacking the Common Core State Standards years ago and have worked hard to align their curriculum with the new standards. Some teachers—perhaps content area colleagues—may be looking at them closely for the first time. In our experience, it takes multiple reviews of the CCSS to arrive at a full understanding of the writing standards because they need to be approached from multiple perspectives. Start by analyzing what is in the standards, followed closely by noticing what is not.

What Are the Common Core State Standards for Writing?

We begin with the anchor standards. All grade-level standards and subject standards are anchored to these ten standards, as shown in Figure 1.2.

Figure 1.2 Common Core Anchor Standards in Writing

Online 1.2
Common Core Anchor Standards in Writing

Text Types and Purposes

1. Write arguments to support claims in an analysis of substantive topics or texts, using valid reasoning and relevant and sufficient evidence.
2. Write informative/explanatory texts to examine and convey complex ideas and information clearly and accurately through the effective selection, organization, and analysis of content.
3. Write narratives to develop real or imagined experiences or events using effective technique, well-chosen details, and well-structured event sequences.

Production and Distribution of Writing

4. Produce clear and coherent writing in which the development, organization, and style are appropriate to task, purpose, and audience.
5. Develop and strengthen writing as needed by planning, revising, editing, rewriting, or trying a new approach.
6. Use technology, including the Internet, to produce and publish writing and to interact and collaborate with others.

Research to Build and Present Knowledge

7. Conduct short as well as more sustained research projects based on focused questions, demonstrating understanding of the subject under investigation.
8. Gather relevant information from multiple print and digital sources, assess the credibility and accuracy of each source, and integrate the information while avoiding plagiarism.
9. Draw evidence from literary or informational texts to support analysis, reflection, and research.

Range of Writing

10. Write routinely over extended time frames (time for research, reflection, and revision) and shorter time frames (a single sitting or a day or two) for a range of tasks, purposes, and audiences.

The first question is "What kind of writing is in the standards?" The answer is quite clear:

1. argument writing
2. informative/explanatory writing
3. narrative writing.

These distinctions are somewhat artificial. In real-world writing, there are no "pure" forms of these modes. For example, sometimes people tell a story to make an argument. Narratives almost always use description to create setting and character. And it is impossible to make an argument on a topic with which readers are not familiar unless informative writing is included.

Today, writing instructors emphasize teaching "the rhetorical situation" rather than the four modes (exposition, description, narration, and argumentation). We will discuss rhetoric in more detail in Chapter 2. For now, let's define the modes that are emphasized in the Common Core State Standards:

1. Argumentative writing seeks to persuade the audience of the position presented.
2. Informative/explanatory texts simply inform the audience or explain a concept to them.
3. Narrative writing tells a story.

Teachers have grown accustomed to preparing students for writing an on-demand, argumentative essay for the SAT or ACT test. The prompts for these writing tests present an issue and ask students to argue for or against it. Because students cannot use any outside materials, they draw from their own experiences and opinion.

That is not the kind of argument that the CCSS call for. Looking carefully at the language of this standard reveals that the argument is embedded in an analysis of "substantive topics or texts." In other words, before writing an argument, students may be asked to read and analyze a text. The claims made in the argument are to be supported by "relevant and sufficient evidence" and connected to the claim using "valid reasoning," all drawn from texts that are provided in the assessment.

Another fundamental difference about the Common Core State Standards is their vertical nature. The wording of each standard changes in the next higher grade level. Teachers now have greater accessibility to knowing what is happening (or should be happening) from grade to grade in terms of what is expected of students. In Figure 1.3, we examine how the writing standards change from sixth grade to twelfth grade. The material

Figure 1.3 CCSS Writing Anchor Standard #1: Write Arguments to Support Claims in an Analysis of Substantive Topics or Texts, Using Valid Reasoning and Relevant and Sufficient Evidence

Sixth grade	Seventh grade	Eighth grade
Introduce claim(s) and organize the reasons and evidence clearly.	Introduce claim(s), *acknowledge alternate or opposing claims*, and organize the reasons and evidence *logically*.	Introduce claim(s), acknowledge and *distinguish the claim(s) from alternate or opposing claims*, and organize the reasons and evidence logically.
Ninth/Tenth grade		**Eleventh/Twelfth grade**
Introduce *precise* claim(s), distinguish the claim(s) from alternate or opposing claims, and *create an organization that establishes clear relationships among claim(s), counterclaims, reasons, and evidence.*		Introduce precise, *knowledgeable* claim(s), *establish the significance of the claim(s)*, distinguish the claim(s) from alternate or opposing claims, and create an organization that *logically sequences* claim(s), counterclaims, reasons, and evidence.

that is "new" at each grade level is in italics. We will start with Writing Standard #1 and look at how the first part of the standard becomes increasingly complex as students move through grades 6–12.

When we look at the vertical progression of this part of Standard #1, we see that the difference between expectations for sixth-grade students and seventh-grade students is that seventh graders are expected to "acknowledge alternate or opposing claims" and use logic to organize their reasons and evidence. Eighth graders must not only acknowledge opposing claims, but also distinguish them from their own claim(s). Ninth and tenth graders must have "precise" claims and establish "clear relationships among claim(s), counterclaims, reasons, and evidence." In eleventh and twelfth grades, students' claims must not only be precise, they must be knowledgeable. Furthermore, the way they organize the relationships among claim(s), counterclaims, reasons, and evidence must be "logically sequenced." In summary, students will be writing arguments throughout grades 6–12, but the skills that are needed to write those arguments—in this case, the use of claims—are expected to develop in specific ways each year. The incremental changes require teachers to have a good grasp of the principles of logic and argumentation.

Okay, we have worked through only one substandard (there are five) of the first standard (there are ten). This means that a writing curriculum has to attend to fifty different grade-level–to–grade-level shifts in the teaching of writing. This is why we said that it takes time and multiple reviews to really get to know the standards.

Our complete chart with the grade-level changes highlighted can be found in our online resources.

Online 1.3
*Chart of Grade
Level Changes
in the Common
Core Writing
Standards*

PLC ACTIVITY

In your PLC or other group, do an analysis of how one of the standards changes from grade to grade. You and your colleagues can work collaboratively to analyze the grade-level changes. After focusing on what changes, collect student writing samples that you believe show the mastery of these new skills. Read through these samples together. If you are not seeing the change you expect to see in student writing, what changes could you make to your curriculum?

What Are the Common Core State Standards for Reading?

A fundamental difference between the CCSS performance assessment (essay test) and all previous essay writing tests is that the CCSS writing assessment also tests reading skills. Therefore, let us examine the reading anchor standards (see Figure 1.4). Compare these reading standards with the description of shifts shown in Figure 1.1. Are there other parts of these reading standards that will require a shift in teaching?

Note the verbs used in these reading standards: determine, summarize, analyze, assess, integrate, delineate, and evaluate. These standards are about much more than comprehension. These higher-order thinking skills, not surprisingly, are not easily demonstrated in traditional objective tests. Students have to write to demonstrate that they have met these standards. For example, here is a question from the Smarter Balanced Assessment Consortium (SBAC) Practice Test released on May 29, 2013, that addresses Standard #1: "Read closely to determine what the text says explicitly and to make logical inferences

Figure 1.4 Common Core Anchor Standards in Reading

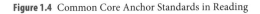

Online 1.4
Common Core Anchor Standards in Reading

Key Ideas and Details

1. Read closely to determine what the text says explicitly and to make logical inferences from it; cite specific textual evidence when writing or speaking to support conclusions drawn from the text.
2. Determine central ideas or themes of a text and analyze their development; summarize the key supporting details and ideas.
3. Analyze how and why individuals, events, or ideas develop and interact over the course of a text.

Craft and Structures

4. Interpret words and phrases as they are used in a text, including determining technical, connotative, and figurative meanings, and analyze how specific word choices shape meaning or tone.
5. Analyze the structure of texts, including how specific sentences, paragraphs, and larger portions of the text (e.g., a section, chapter, scene, or stanza) relate to each other and the whole.
6. Assess how point of view or purpose shapes the content and style of a text.

Integration of Knowledge and Ideas

7. Integrate and evaluate content presented in diverse formats and media, including visually and quantitatively, as well as in words.
8. Delineate and evaluate the argument and specific claims in a text, including the validity of the reasoning as well as the relevance and sufficiency of the evidence.
9. Analyze how two or more texts address similar themes or topics in order to build knowledge or to compare the approaches the authors take.

Range of Reading and Level of Text Complexity

10. Read and comprehend complex literary and informational texts independently and proficiently.

from it; cite specific textual evidence when writing or speaking to support conclusions drawn from the text." This question follows a reading selection about fashion:

> 8. How has consumer demand for sustainable clothing impacted companies? Use at least two details from the text to support your answer.

Type your answer in the space provided.

The point here is that in the era of CCSS, students are not only writing on demand for the performance task (like an essay), they are also writing (and reading) on demand to demonstrate proficiency in reading standards.

In addition to the writing and reading standards, there are language standards that also should be considered when preparing students for writing on demand. We will discuss those next.

What Are the Common Core State Standards for Language?

The language standards are not really new, except for the italicized portion of number 6. English teachers we work with were puzzled by the phrase "domain-specific words," but eventually interpreted it to mean vocabulary specific to the various disciplines that are

Online 1.5
*Common
Core Anchor
Standards in
Language*

Figure 1.5 Common Core Anchor Standards in Language

Conventions of Standard English

1. Demonstrate command of the conventions of standard English grammar and usage when writing or speaking.
2. Demonstrate command of the conventions of standard English capitalization, punctuation, and spelling when writing.

Knowledge of Language

3. Apply knowledge of language to understand how language functions in different contexts, to make effective choices for meaning or style, and to comprehend more fully when reading or listening.

Vocabulary Acquisition and Use

4. Determine or clarify the meaning of unknown and multiple-meaning words and phrases by using context clues, analyzing meaningful word parts, and consulting general and specialized reference materials, as appropriate.
5. Demonstrate understanding of word relationships and nuances in word meanings.
6. *Acquire and use accurately a range of general academic and domain-specific words and phrases sufficient for reading, writing, speaking, and listening at the college and career readiness level;* demonstrate independence in gathering vocabulary knowledge when encountering an unknown term important to comprehension or expression.

now using the same literacy standards—history, science, and technical subjects. The other thing to note about number 6 is the emphasis on "college and career readiness level." This is a reference to the level of text complexity that we saw in the reading standards.

Using Bloom's Taxonomy to Analyze the Common Core Standards

When we have unpacked the standards with teachers, one of our activities has been to highlight the key words in these standards and compare them with Bloom's revised taxonomy of cognitive skills in order to understand the difference in cognitive skills required. After we analyze the standards in this way, it is clear that shifting to CCSS does not mean business as usual.

A list of cognitive activities of each level of Bloom's taxonomy follows. We have highlighted in bold those that are mentioned in the CCSS. Note that we have added some verbs to this taxonomy—they are placed in brackets. For example, the standards do not use the word *assess*, so we added it to the category "evaluate" because they are very similar.

Structure of the Cognitive Process Dimension of the Revised Taxonomy

1) *Remember:* Retrieving relevant knowledge from long-term memory.

    1.1 Recognizing

    1.2 Recalling

2) ***Understand***: Determining the meaning of instructional messages, including oral, written, and graphic communication.

    2.1 Interpreting

    2.2 Exemplifying

    2.3 Classifying

    2.4 ***Summarizing***

    2.5 ***Inferring***

    2.6 ***Comparing***

    2.7 ***Explaining***

3) *Apply:* Carrying out or using a procedure in a given situation.

    3.1 Executing

    3.2 Implementing

4) ***Analyze:*** Breaking material into its constituent parts and detecting how the parts relate to one another and to an overall structure or purpose.

    4.1 Differentiating

    4.2 ***Organizing***

    4.3 Attributing

    [***Delineating***]

5) ***Evaluate:*** Making judgments based on criteria and standards.

    5.1 Checking

    5.2 Critiquing

    [***Assessing***]

    [***Arguing***]

    [***Concluding***]

    [***Reflecting***]

Online 1.6
Structure of the Cognitive Process Dimension of the Revised Taxonomy

6) ***Create:*** Putting elements together to form a novel, coherent whole or make an original product.

    6.1 Generating

    6.2 ***Planning***

    6.3 ***Producing***

    [***Revising***]

    [***Integrating***]

    (Krathwohl 2002)

Figure 1.6 Bloom's Taxonomy Applied to Common Core Anchor Standards

Online 1.7
Bloom's Taxonomy Applied to Common Core Anchor Standards

Common Core Anchor Standards in Reading	Common Core Anchor Standards in Writing
Key Ideas and Details	**Text Types and Purposes**
1. Read closely to determine what the text says explicitly and to make logical **infer**ences from it; cite specific textual evidence when writing or speaking to support **conclusions** drawn from the text.	1. Write **arguments** to support claims in an analysis of substantive topics or texts, using valid reasoning and relevant and sufficient evidence.
2. Determine central ideas or themes of a text and **analyze** their development; **summarize** the key supporting details and ideas.	2. Write informative/**explanatory** texts to examine and convey complex ideas and information clearly and accurately through the effective selection, **organization**, and **analysis** of content.
3. **Analyze** how and why individuals, events, or ideas develop and interact over the course of a text.	3. **Write narratives** to develop real or imagined experiences or events using effective technique, well-chosen details, and well-structured event sequences.
Craft and Structure	**Production and Distribution of Writing**
4. **Interpret** words and phrases as they are used in a text, including determining technical, connotative, and figurative meanings, and **analyze** how specific word choices shape meaning or tone.	4. **Produce** clear and coherent writing in which the development, **organization**, and style are appropriate to task, purpose, and audience.
5. **Analyze** the structure of texts, including how specific sentences, paragraphs, and larger portions of the text (e.g., a section, chapter, scene, or stanza) relate to each other and the whole.	5. Develop and strengthen writing as needed by **planning**, **revising**, editing, rewriting, or trying a new approach.

(continues)

Figure 1.6 Bloom's Taxonomy Applied to Common Core Anchor Standards *(continued)*

Craft and Structure	Production and Distribution of Writing
6. **Assess** how point of view or purpose shapes the content and style of a text.	6. Use technology, including the Internet, to **produce** and publish writing and to interact and collaborate with others.
Integration of Knowledge and Ideas	**Research to Build and Present Knowledge**
7. **Integrate** and **evaluate** content presented in diverse formats and media, including visually and quantitatively, as well as in words.	7. Conduct short as well as more sustained research projects based on focused questions, demonstrating **understand**ing of the subject under investigation.
8. **Delineate** and **evaluate** the argument and specific claims in a text, including the validity of the reasoning as well as the relevance and sufficiency of the evidence.	8. Gather relevant information from multiple print and digital sources, **assess** the credibility and accuracy of each source, and **integrate** the information while avoiding plagiarism.
9. **Analyze** how two or more texts address similar themes or topics in order to build knowledge or to **compare** the approaches the authors take.	9. Draw evidence from literary or informational texts to support **analysis**, **reflection**, and research.
Range of Reading and Level of Text Complexity	**Range of Writing**
10. Read and **comprehend** complex literary and informational texts independently and proficiently.	10. Write routinely over extended time frames (time for research, **reflection**, and **revision**) and shorter time frames (a single sitting or a day or two) for a range of tasks, purposes, and audiences.

Perhaps the most astounding realization from this analysis is that there is no mention of the "lowest" level of Bloom's taxonomy in the standards—remembering. For teachers who feel that Common Core is another demand piled up on their already full plates, it can be a relief to know that some things are not expected—for example, quizzes on the parts of speech or matching tests that require students to remember who the characters were in a novel they read. That does not mean that characters and parts of speech should be absent from teaching, but rather that they emerge on higher cognitive levels, such as asking students to analyze an author's use of verbs in a strong passage of writing or asking students to compare and contrast two characters for the purpose of illuminating a theme in a novel.

The other pattern that jumps out is that the writing standards have a lot more words that belong to the category highest on Bloom's taxonomy: to create. This is not surprising; writing is a highly creative act, and it is cognitively challenging. Writing skills cannot be assessed through traditional objective test items—it takes a performance task, like writing an essay.

Notes on College Readiness: *What Is Missing from the Common Core State Standards?*

If you have compared your pre-CCSS curriculum to the Common Core State Standards, you probably noticed that some important topics are missing. We have, too, and so have our professional organizations. In fact, three of them—the National Council of Teachers of English (NCTE), the National Writing Project (NWP), and the Council of Writing Program Administrators (WPA)—worked quickly and collaboratively to write their own explanation of what it means to be "college and career ready" in a "Framework for Success in Postsecondary Writing" (2011). See Figure 1.7. You can download a free PDF of this framework from our online resources or request a hardcopy. Most of the habits of mind and experiences in the Framework are notably lacking in the CCSS; nevertheless, they are essential for college and career readiness. In fact, it is through cultivating these habits of mind, not drilling students in the standards, that teachers will best help students contend with the new assessments and life beyond secondary school.

Online 1.8
Framework for Success in Postsecondary Writing: Summary Chart

Online 1.9
Framework for Success in Postsecondary Writing: Full Document

Figure 1.7 Framework for Success in Postsecondary Writing

Habits of Mind	Writing, Reading, and Critical Analysis Experiences
Curiosity	Rhetorical knowledge
Openness	Critical thinking
Engagement	Writing processes
Creativity	Knowledge of conventions
Persistence	Ability to compose in multiple
Responsibility	environments
Flexibility	
Metacognition	

Putting the Common Core State Standards in Context: Our Driving Metaphor

Unpacking the standards can leave us feeling anxious, so we want to use a metaphor to put them in a more manageable place.

Kelly's son, Alex, turned fourteen this year and has been eager to get a learner's permit so he can start learning to drive a car. As teachers of teenagers, you know how important this step is for adolescents (and how terrifying it is for parents!).

To get the permit, Alex has to study the driver's education manual and pass a written test to demonstrate that he understands the rules of the road. He will soon be logging as many hours as his mom's stomach can withstand to get the experience he needs to pass the test to get his driver's license.

There is a fundamental difference between the learner's permit test and the driver's test: In the former, only a written test is required; in the latter one has to actually get in the car and drive. That is why the driver's test is considered a *performance* test. It tests not only the driver's knowledge of the rules of the road, but also the driver's ability to apply that knowledge in an actual car, on an actual road.

After a driver passes this test, he or she is deemed fit to use our roads and highways with everyone else. But does this mean that everyone with a driver's license is a good driver? No. Newly licensed drivers need additional independent practice to develop their skills. And even people who have been driving for a long time don't necessarily have the greatest skills—when was the last time you saw a driver turn without using a turn signal, or pass you at 20 mph over the speed limit? A driver's license merely means that someone has met the minimum standards necessary to obtain a license to drive.

The performance part of the driving test is usually done in quiet conditions, in little to no traffic, and in good driving conditions. True, it is a nerve-wracking experience for most, but it is a far cry from driving in snow or in a big city during rush hour. As a society, we are counting on drivers continuing to gain experience after they get that first license so that they will be able to apply those skills to a variety of settings.

How a Driver's Test Is Similar to the CCSS Assessments

The new assessments for the Common Core State Standards are much like a driver's test. Everyone needs to pass them to demonstrate they have the requisite writing skills to be successful in college and in their careers. The multiple-choice parts of the tests are like the driver's permit test on the information in the driver's manual. The part where students write an essay (or essays) is like the actual driving—it is the performance part of the test. As with the driving part of the test, the writing part of the common core assessment should be preceded by hours and hours of practice.

What if we prepared drivers for their tests by having them go over and over the driver's course on blacktop in back of the Department of Motor Vehicles? They would be really good at driving that course come test day, right? Sure, they would, but what about the first time they pull into traffic? Or come to an intersection where the traffic lights are out? They would fall apart and become a menace to other drivers.

It is not enough for drivers to have hours and hours of practice before taking their driver's test. They need to have lots of practice in a *variety* of conditions, which teaches the flexibility (and flexibility is one of those college readiness "habits of mind") to deal with new situations. It is the same with writers—they need lots and lots of practice, not just in the kind of writing they will face in a timed writing test, but lots of practice in a variety of situations.

You may feel uncomfortable when you get into a new car (like a rental at the airport), but you can probably still drive it if you take a few moments to familiarize yourself with the controls. This is because we know that all cars have certain things in common—a steering wheel, brakes, gears, turn signals, and so forth. Similarly, writers who know the things that all writing situations have in common—an audience, a purpose, a context, a format—may feel a bit uncomfortable the first time they are asked to write for an unfamiliar situation, but if they have rhetorical knowledge they should be able to figure it out. Sure, the window wipers might come on the first time we try to turn, but that is soon remedied.

However, some skills have to be automatic. Drivers can't be thinking each time, "Now press the clutch, now gently brake." Similarly, writers can't be thinking, "Put in a topic sentence, make sure your sentence is complete." Some moves need to be so well learned that students no longer need a teacher to tell them those things—they are automatic. Engaging students in metacognitive lessons will help these skills become automatic.

What Is Writing on Demand?

For secondary school students, the ability to write effectively on demand is an increasingly important skill. Indeed, much of the writing done "on the job" is writing on demand—email messages, memos, estimates for a job to be completed, proposals for projects, summaries of meetings, social media postings, text messages, and so forth. Writing on demand is also required in colleges and universities. For example, some college students have to write dozens of essay exams over the course of their college career, not to mention the ubiquitous email messages to professors, collaborative projects with peers, and on and on. For some students, timed writing exams can be barriers to college entrance, to progression through required courses, and to teacher certification when qualifying scores on the Praxis exams are needed to complete the degree.

Writing using social media such as blogs is, in many cases, a kind of on-demand writing that is widely read and commented on. The comments themselves are also typically composed in a single sitting. Those with the writing skills to comment on current events in a short time frame can be highly influential in our highly mediated world; think of the enormous funds raised online and through text messaging for relief after the earthquake in Haiti and the devastation caused by Hurricane Sandy. According to *The Guardian*, bloggers "help elect presidents and take down attorney generals while simultaneously celebrating the minutiae of our everyday obsessions" (March 9, 2008).

In the twenty-first century, writing is more important than ever, and everyone is writing more. Although it is important to prepare students for the CCSS assessments, it is even more important to help them become capable and confident writers for whom writing on demand is just one of the many writing challenges they can meet.

Chapter Two

Understanding the Language of Writing Assessments

CHAPTER OVERVIEW *This chapter provides strategies for:*

- *identifying key terms*

- *unpacking text complexity*

- *understanding different types of assessment questions*

- *developing strategies for responding to questions.*

*I*n one way, it's a simple thing: the writing assessments for the Common Core State Standards (CCSS) will determine whether students can actually produce writing that is well grounded and effective for a variety of audiences and purposes. At the same time, a lot of meanings are packed into that goal. This chapter will unpack those meanings by exploring the language of writing assessment.

Before we look at specific terms, however, we want to underscore the importance and value of sharing this information with students. Too often students experience assessment as something that is done *to* them; something that, like Oz, is hidden behind a curtain of secrecy; something that is capricious and arbitrary. School hallways echo with questions like "Whadjdya get?" and answers like "She gave me a C," that reflect the feelings of confusion and alienation many students have about assessment.

We have found that one of the most effective ways to help students improve as writers and to prepare them for any writing assessment is to make assessment a visible and regular part of classroom experience. By this we don't mean subjecting students to weeks and weeks of test preparation. To be sure, it is a good idea for students to be familiar with the kind of writing they will be expected to do on a high-stakes test, but a better option than lengthy test prep is to help students understand the relationship between writing and assessment, which means, among other things, understanding the standards by which their writing will be assessed.

Introducing Some Key Terms

Assessment has its own language, and it includes a number of terms that are unfamiliar to students. One of the first ways teachers can help students understand assessment is to help them learn some of its vocabulary. Students who become familiar with the terms used in assessment are often able to move toward better thinking about their own ways of learning as they develop writing skills. Figure 2.1 includes a number of terms that students can benefit from understanding. The CCSS have brought some new concepts and terms into the language of assessment, so we have included them as well as more familiar terms.

In many cases the definitions offered in the figure do not do justice to the full meaning of the term, and later in this book we explain the terms more fully. In such cases, the figure simply calls attention to terms for which a more extended meaning will be offered later.

Online 2.1
*Common CCSS
Assessment
Terms*

Figure 2.1 Common CCSS Assessment Terms

Term	Definition	Example
Analytical essay	An essay that explains ideas in one or more texts, is supported by evidence, and is logically developed	Compare the perspectives on race in *To Kill a Mockingbird* and *Black Boy*.
Constructed response	An assessment that provides information that students use to answer questions	Read the following first paragraph of an argumentative text that lacks a clear claim and rewrite it to make the claim clear.
Formative assessment	Assessment that occurs during the writing process and provides feedback that can be used in further writing but does not result in a grade or score	Peer response, a teacher-student conference, or written comments on a draft all provide formative assessment.
High-stakes test	A single test that controls a life-shaping event, such as passing to the next grade or graduating from high school	District-mandated or state mandated tests

Figure 2.1 Common CCSS Assessment Terms *(continued)*

Term	Definition	Example
Performance task	Assessment that gives students opportunities to display knowledge or skills rather than simply choose a single answer	Write an explanation of the process of thermodynamics.
Rubric	A guide for evaluating writing that lists features to be considered, along with qualitative dimensions of each, so that distinctions can be made among pieces of writing	CCSS rubric
Selected response	Students select an answer from among several choices given.	Multiple-choice test; true-false test
Short answer	Brief written response to a text-based question	Write an explanation of the details that support the answer given above.
Summative assessment	Assessment that occurs at the end of a period of instruction and results in a grade or score	A final exam, a paper written at the end of a unit, or a state-mandated test could all be summative assessments. For CCSS, summative evaluation will occur near the end of the school year.
Text complexity	As defined by CCSS, it is comprised of a combination of quantitative measures of syntax and vocabulary, qualitative judgments of human readers, and student-teacher interactions.	See discussion that follows.
Text-dependent questions	A prompt that requires students to read closely and draw evidence from the text	After reading *The Story of My Life*, explain how Helen Keller learns language.

The list of terms in Figure 2.1 is not an exhaustive one, but helping students understand terms like these will enable them to look at assessment as part of learning rather than something to fear or resent. It is particularly important to give students access to the language associated with CCSS assessments because those assessments will be part of their experience of schooling.

Text Complexity

One of the most prominent terms in the CCSS is *text complexity*, and it is important to writing instruction because a key feature emphasized by the CCSS is the relationship between reading and writing. Of the ten anchor standards for writing in the CCSS, three of them connect writing and reading directly by referring to analysis of texts, gathering information from multiple texts, and drawing evidence from texts. Furthermore, most of the sample writing prompts released by PARCC and Smarter Balanced—the two consortia charged with developing assessments for CCSS—require substantive reading. Accordingly, it is useful to think about the implications of text complexity for writers.

Online 2.2
Text Complexity in Appendix A of the CCSS

The CCSS definition of text complexity is the "level of meaning, structure, language conventionality and clarity, knowledge demands, word frequency, sentence length [all in the context of] student knowledge, motivation, and interest" (a link to Appendix A of the CCSS, where text complexity is discussed on page 4, is included in our online materials). As this definition makes clear, this version of text complexity includes multiple features, and the CCSS appendix further elaborates its meaning in a three-part model that includes qualitative dimensions, quantitative dimensions, and reader-task considerations.

Quantitative features include aspects of texts that can be most easily discerned with the aid of digital tools and algorithms, features such as the variety and difficulty of the vocabulary used, and the length and syntactic complexity of sentences. By themselves, these features, sometimes referred to as lexiles or readability measures, do not offer definitive indications of appropriate texts for students, but they do provide useful information that can be used to help students become more aware of their own use of vocabulary and syntax. Students can examine two texts that score very differently in quantitative terms to find out how their sentence structures vary and to compare the kinds of words used in each. This analysis can be used to inform the way they construct sentences in their own writing. Students can use a free online program like Coh-Metrix (a link to the Coh-Metrix website is included in our online materials) to analyze vocabulary and a number of syntactic features in their own writing.

Online 2.3
Coh-Metrix Text Analysis

Qualitative features are described this way by CCSS: "In the Standards qualitative measures, along with professional judgment in matching a text to reader and task, serve as a necessary complement and sometimes as a corrective to quantitative measures, which … cannot (at least at present) capture all of the elements that make a text easy or challenging to read and are not equally successful in rating the complexity of all categories of text" (Appendix A, p. 5). CCSS offers four qualitative measures of text complexity:

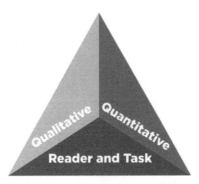

1. *Levels of meaning (literary texts) or purpose (informational texts).* Literary texts with a single level of meaning tend to be easier to read than literary texts with multiple levels of meaning (such as satires, in which the author's literal message is intentionally at odds with his or her underlying message). Similarly, informational texts with an explicitly stated purpose are generally easier to comprehend than informational texts with an implicit, hidden, or obscure purpose.

2. *Structure.* Texts of low complexity tend to have simple, well-marked, and conventional structures, whereas texts of high complexity tend to have complex, implicit, and (particularly in literary texts) unconventional structures. Simple literary texts tend to relate events in chronological order, while complex literary texts make more frequent use of flashbacks, flash-forwards, and other manipulations of time and sequence. Simple informational texts are likely not to deviate from the conventions of common genres and subgenres, while complex informational texts are likely not to conform to the norms and conventions of a specific discipline. Graphics tend to be simple and either unnecessary or merely supplementary to the meaning of texts of low complexity, whereas texts of high complexity tend to have similarly complex graphics

whose interpretation is essential to understanding the text and which provide an independent source of information within a text.

3. *Language conventionality and clarity.* Texts that rely on literal, clear, contemporary, and conversational language tend to be easier to read than texts that rely on figurative, ironic, ambiguous, purposefully misleading, archaic, or otherwise unfamiliar language or on academic and domain-specific vocabulary.

4. *Knowledge demands.* Texts that make few assumptions about the extent of readers' life experiences and the depth of their cultural/literary and content/discipline knowledge are generally less complex than texts that make many assumptions in one or more of these areas. These are features that teachers regularly consider when thinking about appropriate texts for students. Their conversations are filled with concerns about how to help students discern the author's purpose, inferred versus literal meanings, and ambiguity.

As is true for quantitative dimensions of text complexity, students can benefit from using these four criteria to consider relative levels of complexity in texts they read. In turn, students can use the same criteria to consider the qualitative complexity of their own writing.

The third feature of the three-part model of text complexity, reader-task considerations, focuses on the aspects of student knowledge, motivation, and interests referred to in the definition. As CCSS Appendix A puts it, "harder texts may be appropriate for highly knowledgeable or skilled readers, and easier texts may be suitable as an expedient for building struggling readers' knowledge or reading skill up to the level required by the Standards. Highly motivated readers are often willing to put in the extra effort required to read harder texts that tell a story or contain information in which they are deeply interested" (Appendix A, p. 7). Helping students understand this dimension of text complexity can heighten their understanding of the importance of thinking about audience in writing.

Helping students to understand text complexity is an essential part of preparing them for CCSS assessments because reading plays such a central role in CCSS assessments of writing. The texts students are asked to read as part of these assessments are challenging, and students will benefit from having a language to discuss the reading they encounter.

RESEARCH AND POLITICAL CONSIDERATIONS

Secondary school faculties rarely think of themselves as teachers of reading, but the CCSS emphasis on text complexity requires teachers to reconsider this position. If students are going to succeed in CCSS assessments, they will need support in learning strategies for reading a variety of literary and informational texts.

An NCTE policy research brief, titled "Reading Instruction for *All* Students," suggests a number of research-based strategies, including these:

- Recognize the role that motivation plays in students' reading by modeling for students how to engage with complex texts that do and do not interest them.

- Engage students in performative reading responses such as gesture, mime, vocal intonation, characterization, and dramatization to enable active construction of meaning and construct a collaborative environment that builds on the strengths of individual students.

- Have students read multiple texts focused on the same topic to improve comprehension through text-to-text connections.

- Foster students' engagement with complex texts by teaching students how different textual purposes, genres, and modes require different strategies for reading.

- Encourage students to choose texts, including nonfiction, for themselves, in addition to assigned ones, to help them see themselves as capable readers who can independently use reading capabilities they learn in class.

- Demonstrate, especially at the secondary level, how digital and visual texts, including multimodal and multigenre texts, require different approaches to reading.

- Connect students' reading of complex texts with their writing about reading and with writing that uses complex texts as models so they will recognize and be able to negotiate many different types of complex texts.

- Develop students' ability to engage in meaningful discussion of the complex texts they read in whole-class, small group, and partner conversations so they can learn to negotiate and comprehend complex texts independently.

A link to the entire brief is included in our online materials.

Online 2.4
"Reading Instruction for All Students" by NCTE

Understanding Various Kinds of Questions

The CCSS assessments in writing include several kinds of questions, each structured a bit differently and each requiring a different sort of response from students. Much of the Smarter Balanced assessment will take the form of computer-adaptive tests (CAT), where the computer program adjusts the difficulty of questions as students are taking the test. For example, if a student answers a question correctly, the next question will be more challenging, but if the student responds incorrectly, the next question will be easier. The PARCC questions will also be administered online, but these will not be computer adaptive tests.

Selected-Response Items

Both PARCC and Smarter Balanced Assessment Consortium (SBAC) assessments include some selected-response or multiple-choice items to assess writing. Some of these will focus on issues of vocabulary and usage such as:

> What does the word *calculate* mean in the following sentence?
>
> Esther could easily calculate the resolutions she had made.
>
> a. remember   b. count   c. forget   d. number

Most students will not have difficulty with items like these because, in the above case, they will recognize that calculate means "count," that *easily* is an adverb, but it can be helpful to have them explain *how* they know the correct answer. This process of thinking about their own ways of knowing, or metacognition, offers students another perspective on assessment. Metacognition can help students understand more fully how they can use their own knowledge in responding to the questions required of them. This kind of thinking can also help students with more complicated selected-response items, such as the following.

> Use the keyboard to correct any spelling and punctuation errors you find in the following passage.
>
> Soccer is fun because you have to run alot. My coach Sam Washburn likes me to play in the foreward position and I like that too.

This item is not terribly difficult, but it requires students to take a more active stance and recognize misspellings like *alot* and *foreward*, and to insert commas around the proper name, between the two independent clauses, and before the word *too*. Here, as in the previous case, asking students to analyze how they approach an item like this and to explain what kind of knowledge it requires will expand their understanding of assessment. Furthermore, giving students opportunities to edit one another's writing as part of the process of writing (see Chapter 4, Improving the Writing: Revision, Editing, Proofreading) will enable them to see the connection between assessing the writing of one of their peers and being tested on their own ability to identify errors in writing.

The following selected response question is more challenging even though it takes multiple-choice form.

> *Directions:* Rephrase the following according to the directions given, and choose the response that best corresponds to the necessary changes to the original sentence. Keep the meaning of the sentence as close to the original as possible, maintaining natural phrasing, the requirements of standard written English, and logical and concise construction.
>
> 1. Subsequent references to the man are absent; this has always been considered puzzling and conspicuous.
>   Begin with *The absence*
>
>   a. the man has always
>   b. references have always
>   c. puzzling has always
>   d. the man considered
>   e. the man puzzled

The rephrased sentence would read: "The absence of subsequent references to the man has always been considered puzzling and conspicuous," and the correct answer to this item is, of course, option a. Students who are strong writers and have many opportunities to revise their own writing, as well as make substantive feedback on their peers' writing, will do well on this kind of question.

Classroom Moves

To help students develop their metacognitive capacities, ask them to write a detailed explanation of how they arrived at an answer for a sample item. The sample here, based on the previous item, illustrates what such a narrative might look like.

My Thinking

I read through the sentence and then looked at *The absence*. In my mind I tried to think how the sentence would go if *The absence* came first. Then I scanned the possible answers and eliminated *d* and *e*. I tried to imagine the rest of the sentence and decided *The absence* would have to be followed by *of subsequent references to the man*. Then I realized that *this* wouldn't belong in the sentence anymore and I could get rid of the semicolon. I looked at the rest of the sentence and realized that it could stay the same because *The absence* had become the subject of the sentence and verb *has* would agree with it.

Putting the rest of the sentence together helped me eliminate *b* and *c*, so then I knew that *a* was the answer.

Writing a narrative like this can help students see how to think through the various choices presented by selected response items, to understand how items like this are constructed, and to consider how they might respond to them. It can be especially helpful for students to compare their own accounts with those of their peers to get a fuller sense of various ways to approach selected response items and, thereby, to understand this kind of assessment more fully.

After students have written and compared some accounts of the ways they think when they are answering selected response items, they can take this process to the next level by figuring out what literacy skills they need to do the thinking that items like these require. This process helps students think about the skills and knowledge they draw on as they write. Students can begin to identify their own literacy skills if they look at each cognitive move in turn. For example, the account about the "absence" sentence begins by describing a process of reading and then moves on to describe a mental rearrangement of the sentence. Students typically do best when they analyze a peer's account of thinking processes. This exercise helps them simultaneously do better on tests and become better learners because they gain insight into what it takes to be successful on writing tests. Here, for example, is a list of the literacy skills necessary to do the thinking described in "My Thinking" in an effort to answer the "absence" question:

- reading and comprehending written passages
- rearranging components of a sentence
- identifying wrong answers
- recognizing correct subject-verb agreement

When students can identify the skills necessary for answering assessment items successfully, they can become more intentional about developing those skills. Recognizing, for example, that it is useful to know how to do a mental rearrangement of sentences can make them more receptive to sentence-combining exercises and other strategies that strengthen their ability to write effectively at the sentence level (see Chapter 8).

Other selected response questions ask students to do more complicated thinking, as the following example shows. The excerpt is from a writer's informational paragraph about the Ferris wheel.

Read the paragraph and click on the sentence the writer should revise to maintain a consistent focus.

The first Ferris wheel was built for the World's Fair of 1893. It was a colossus that weighed about 2,100 tons. The diameter of the wheel was 250 feet. Its 36 cars were each as big as a trolley car that could hold 60 people. In one day the Ferris wheel carried 38,000 riders. In all about 1.5 million fair-goers enjoyed the first Ferris wheel. Although the first Ferris wheel was a hit, it did not achieve the lasting fame of the Eiffel Tower. (SBAC grade 11 ELA item from May 29 sample test)

Selected-Response/Text-Based Questions

Although there are some selected-response questions in both SBAC and PARCC assessments that stand alone, a great number require students to read a long passage and answer a number of selected-response questions based on that text. Such questions ask students to identify how certain sentences affect the reader, indicate which sentences support a specific point, contain details that support the main idea of the passage, or identify the meaning of a specific word in the context of the text. Here is an example:

Read the excerpt from the text and the directions that follow.

Our partnership started out just as I thought it would. As soon as we sat down to look at the scene, Luke was pompously proclaiming himself an expert.

What does the word *pompously* mean as it is used in this excerpt?

a. loftily

b. arrogantly

c. dignifiedly

d. magnificently

(SBAC grade 11 item from May 29 ELA test)

Online 2.5
*May 29, 2013
SBAC Sample
ELA Test*

PLC ACTIVITY: INVENTORY OF LITERACY SKILLS IN TEST ITEMS

Select one of the items from the CCSS assessments included here or go to the link to the May 29, 2013 SBAC Sample ELA Test (included in our online materials), and select an item from this test.

Working together, make a list of all the literacy skills students will need to succeed on this item.

Brainstorm ideas for instruction that will address the literacy skills on your list.

Constructed-Response Items/Performance Tasks

Constructed-response items are among the most common in CCSS assessments of writing. These items ask students to do some writing rather than simply identify features in sentences or passages written by others, but, in some cases, not much actual writing is required and the writing is largely shaped by the prompt. For instance, one kind of constructed-response item presents students with a draft of a first paragraph from an argumentative essay and requires students to revise the paragraph to make the central claim clearer. Here is an example from a Smarter Balanced sample test:

A student is writing an argumentative essay about physical education (PE) classes in middle school for her English assignment. The teacher suggested the student add an opening sentence that establishes a clear claim. Read the student's draft and the directions that follow.

Too many kids waste dozens of hours each week in front of the TV or computer. They may be exercising their fingers and sometimes their minds, but they are not exercising the rest of their bodies. But, in physical education class, they do. Recent research has shown that physical education class has many benefits: It can teach teamwork, build confidence, and increase academic success. Students who take regular physical education classes not only develop healthier habits throughout their lives, but the activity reduces anxiety and improves judgment. One study revealed that students who did not have access to these classes were 2.5 times more likely to become inactive. Some students may feel awkward in physical education class; however, they may be getting more out of it than they realize.

Write at least one sentence at the beginning of the paragraph that establishes a clear claim.

To prepare students for writing tasks like the previous one, students need opportunities to work in writing workshops or peer review. Writing workshop (see Chapter 4) also offers a way for students to become better editors. Students who have participated in peer review will be well prepared for this type of item because it calls upon the same ability to assess another student's writing.

Another skill that will help students with constructed responses like the previous one is the ability to analyze the prompt carefully. The single line of instruction contains two words—*claim* and *clear* that are central to what students are required to do in response to this prompt. First, the students need to decide what point the author of "The Internet in Classrooms" is making and then decide what makes the paragraph less than clear.

Helping students do a close and careful reading of the prompt becomes even more important in another kind of constructed-response item. Here students are given a longer text to read and then write in more detail in response to a directive based on the reading. For example, students are asked to read a selection from a biography of Amelia Earhart (the full text of this biography appears in our online materials) and then they are given these directions:

Online 2.6
*Biography of
Amelia Earhart*

Based on the information in the text "Biography of Amelia Earhart," write an essay that summarizes and explains the challenges Earhart faced throughout her life.

Remember to use textual evidence to support your ideas.

Figure 2.2 Common Core State Standards Addressed by This Assessment

Reading Standards	Writing Standards	Language Standards
RI 7.1 Cite several pieces of textual evidence to support analysis of what the text says explicitly as well as inferences drawn from the text.	W 7.2 Write informative/ explanatory texts to examine a topic and convey ideas, concepts, and information through the selection, organization, and analysis of relevant content.	L 7.1 Demonstrate command of the conventions of standard English grammar and usage when writing or speaking.
RI 7.2 Determine two or more central ideas in a text and analyze their development over the course of the text; provide an objective summary of the text.	W 7.9 Draw evidence from literary or informational texts to support analysis, reflection, and research.	L 7.2 Demonstrate command of the conventions of standard English capitalization, punctuation, and spelling when writing. L 7.3 Use knowledge of language and its conventions when writing, speaking, reading, or listening.

This version of constructed response items calls on students' ability to read a text and draw evidence from it in order to write a convincing essay. It also demonstrates the close linkage between Common Core State Standards and the accompanying assessments, as Figure 2.2 makes clear.

This prompt also contains information that can guide students' reading of the text, indicating that they should pay attention to the *challenges* Earhart faces. With the words *summarize* and *explain*, it also tells students what kind of writing they will be expected to do. Learning to do a quick analysis of a prompt prior to reading the designated text will enable students to understand the goals of the assessment and, therefore, to read more effectively, as we learned when we began looking at students' experiences with prompts like these. When students in Alissa Helm's class were asked to respond to this prompt, it became clear that many of them needed help reading and understanding it (see Figure 2.3).

Figure 2.3 Two Seventh Graders' Essays on Amelia Earhart

Online 2.7
Two Seventh Graders' Essays on Amelia Earhart

Amelia Earhart's Challenges
by Malani

Amelia Earhart is considered a leader because she withstood many challenges. In a time where women were considered to be less successful than men, Amelia Earhart continued to reach for her goals. She also did not have all of the financial support she needed. Weather conditions were also a factor in her success. In all of these trials she would keep going.

In Earhart's time men were stereotypically stronger, smarter, and braver than women. That didn't stop her though. It didn't matter to her what people said, she wanted to inspire women. She proved that she could do anything she set her mind to.

Earhart also needed more money than she had. She faced financial challenges many times. She continued to reach her goals. Even though at times it may have been hard she always found the money she needed. Earhart didn't let any financial trials stop her from becoming the legend she is today.

Weather could also make her missions hard to complete. It didn't faze her though, she would keep on going. It could be cloudy and windy but she would still fly despite the conditions.

Thanks to Amelia Earhart women are considered to be more equal to men than ever before. She withstood many challenges and shows that you can do anything you set your mind to. That makes her a leader.

Summary
by John

She was 10 years old when Earhart saw her first plane. She hadn't really liked it, so not until December 28, 1920, did Amelia first tried to ride a plane; with a man named Frank Hawks. After that experience she wanted to become a pilot as well, someday. After that she became a tomboy, exploring, climbing trees, and hunting.

Earhart attended many schools and jobs. First, was Hyde Park High School, then was doctoring school where she became a nurse, next was college, finally she went to an aviator school where she first learned to fly. After six months she bought herself a yellow plane. She used this plane to achieve a record by flying 14,000 feet in the air. She was later asked to fly across the Atlantic Ocean, so, of course, she agreed to it. On June 17, 1928, she was back and was greeted with a parade. Amelia even got to meet the president!

One day, Earhart met a man named George Putnam. On February 7, 1931, they became married. Together they wanted (and succeeded) Amelia Earhart to fly across the Atlantic solo; if she succeeded she would the 2nd person to do so and 1st woman. On May 20, 1932, Earhart took off across the Atlantic. On January 11, 1935, she flew across the Pacific.

When Amelia turned 40 years old, she made a plan to fly across the world! So on June 1, 1937, Earhart took off across the world. But, on July 2 at 7:42 am, her plane ran low on fuel. So she sent a transmission to the navy, but they never responded. Finally, they retrieved her stress signal, so they returned the call. But, it was too late. Earhart answered saying her coordinates. But, after that, nothing was ever heard again from Amelia Earhart.

Malani and John approached this task quite differently, as revealed by their titles. Malani's title reflects the prompt's requirement that students focus on the challenges in the reading selection, while John's title reflects his attempt to summarize the entire reading selection. When we looked at the two students' copies of the Earhart biography, we saw how they had highlighted very different details in the reading selection. From this exploration, it became clear that in the era of CCSS, to succeed at writing on demand students have to know how to read both the prompt and accompanying texts effectively.

Although the Earhart biography is a relatively accessible piece of writing, the challenges it describes are both obvious and subtle. The obvious ones can be described as largely technical—the financial constraints along with mechanical and weather conditions that made flying difficult; but less obvious is the persistent challenge posed by gender, for a woman who tried "to do things as men have tried." Discussing passages such as these, with students and identifying the multiple layers of meaning represented by a word like *challenges*, is part of preparing students to analyze prompts effectively and helping them understand the language of writing assessment.

Classroom Moves

In particular, students can benefit from writing and sharing brief descriptions of their processes of reading, answering substantive questions, and explaining where they encountered difficulties with the passage. Students can use this form:

- In three sentences summarize the main points of the passage.
- What was confusing or difficult to understand?
- What words are unfamiliar?

Answering questions like these can help students become more aware of how they read and provide them with strategies for reading the texts that are part of the CCSS assessments. It can also help them write accounts of how they addressed difficulties like these.

In addition to developing reading strategies, students can work on approaches to writing in response to CCSS assessments. It can be useful to have students practice writing in response to prompts that appear in constructed-response items, but we have found that this work is even more effective when combined with asking students to recount how they did that writing. Just as is the case with approaching the reading demands of constructed-response items, students can draw on their own and others' accounts to identify skills necessary to succeed with the writing,

Some of the CCSS assessments will have multiple parts that require students to do research to gather information rather than simply reading assigned selections. Here is an example of this kind of prompt:

> *Classroom Activity* (20 minutes): Using stimuli such as charts and photos, the teacher prepares students for Part 1 of the assessment by leading them in a discussion of the use of nuclear power. Through discussion:
>
> - Students share prior knowledge about nuclear power.
> - Students discuss the use and controversies involving nuclear power.
>
> *Part 1* (50 minutes): Students complete reading and prewriting activities in which:
>
> - They read and take notes on a series of Internet sources about the pros and cons of nuclear power.
> - They respond to two constructed-response questions that ask students to analyze and evaluate the credibility of the arguments in favor and in opposition to nuclear power.
>
> *Part 2* (70 minutes): Students individually compose a full-length argumentative report for their congressperson in which they use textual evidence to justify the position they take, pro or con, on whether a nuclear power plant should be built in their state. (PARCC)

A very effective way to help students prepare for a prompt like this is to do a practice version so they experience all the steps and describe briefly how they accomplished each. Then, they can move to the next level and identify the literacy skills they need to succeed with such a prompt. This process heightens students' capacity for metacognition—the capacity for thinking about their own learning and thinking—because they begin to think about the skills and knowledge they need to draw upon. Students can begin to identify their own literacy skills if they look at each cognitive move in turn, which helps them prepare for tests and become better learners because they gain insight into what it takes to be successful. If students consider the skills necessary to succeed on Parts 1 and 2 above, they will probably generate a list that includes the following items:

- Read and interpret charts and other graphic presentations of information.
- Listen to and learn from peers in a discussion.
- Share personal knowledge about a controversial topic.
- Distinguish between fact and opinion.
- Identify reliable sources of information on the Internet.
- Summarize key points made in an online resource.
- Organize information gathered from several sources.
- Evaluate the credibility of arguments made about a controversial topic.
- Take a clear position on a controversial topic.
- Address a designated audience in writing.
- Use the genre of report effectively.
- Incorporate evidence from multiple sources.
- Produce a convincing evidence-based written argument.

Identifying these specific skills gives students a much more comprehensive understanding of the demands of CCSS assessments of writing. Once students have identified skills like these, they can become more intentional about developing them. Providing opportunities to practice each of these skills, to write explanations of their own processes of doing so, and to share these explanations with peers will enable students to understand and prepare for the CCSS assessments.

In addition, Part 2 of the previous prompt contains key terms that students can analyze to understand more fully what is expected of them. Prompt analysis questions like those that follow offer students a way to unpack the prompt and understand it on a deeper level. Student responses that might stimulate discussion are included with each question.

1. What is the central claim or topic called for?
   My topic is nuclear energy, and I have to take a position on it. Once I've decided on a position, I'll need to consider how I can make the best argument for it.

2. Who is the intended audience?
   I am addressing a congressperson, but I don't know what position this person has on nuclear energy. It would help me to know that.

3. What is the purpose of this writing task?

   I need to persuade the congressperson that we either should or shouldn't build a nuclear power plant in our state.

4. What strategies will be most effective?

   Phrases like *justify the position* tell me that I need to give evidence for my position. I can't just state my opinion.

5. What is my role in achieving the purpose?

   Once I've decided on my position, I'll have to be an advocate for it, emphasizing all the points in favor of it.

Online 2.8
Prompt Analysis Questions

Using these questions can help students take a much closer look at the words in prompts and, in the process, develop a fuller understanding of the language of assessment. Likewise, when students move from answering practice tests, to explaining how they came to their answers, and then to identifying the skills necessary to successfully respond to prompts, they will have a well-developed understanding of the language of assessment. More importantly, they will be developing a deep understanding of their own ways of thinking and writing, a capacity that will serve them well in many contexts of writing.

Chapter Three

Developing Curriculum Materials for the CCSS

CHAPTER OVERVIEW *This chapter provides strategies for:*

- *looking at the big picture of curriculum development*

- *understanding how the Common Core State Standards are impacting curriculum development*

- *getting the most writing improvement out of curriculum changes*

- *incorporating more writing into math class*

- *including more informational texts into lessons*

- *working collaboratively to develop CCSS units*

- *finding resources to support development of curriculum materials.*

When the state of New York shifted to CCSS-based ELA tests, proficiency rates dropped from 55 percent to 31 percent. The response from the NY State Board of Regents was not to increase "test prep," but to put more emphasis on curriculum and instruction (*Education Week*, August 19, 2013). We believe this was a wise move. The CCSS is not a curriculum in and of itself—it takes thoughtful, collaborative work to interpret and implement the standards, which can be addressed in multiple ways. We believe—as does the NCTE, in the position statement that follows—that it is important for teachers to develop curriculum, because they know the students, they know the context, and because they are the ones who will bring the curriculum to life in their daily practice. We also know that working to develop curriculum is challenging, time-consuming, and fraught with many tensions.

Despite the challenges, we advocate that teachers be given the time and opportunity to develop curriculum. Without curriculum planning, it is unlikely students will demonstrate proficiency on the CCSS assessments, or that they will truly be college and career ready. And, most important, without curriculum planning it is unlikely that students will develop the literacy skills they need to lead productive and fulfilling lives.

RESEARCH AND POLITICAL CONSIDERATIONS

NCTE Position Statement: Resolution on Curriculum Development

Background

The education reform movement of the 1980s produced legislation which in the judgment of many NCTE members was often counterproductive to its goal of educational improvement. Be it therefore Resolved, that the National Council of Teachers of English affirm that as professional practitioners, English language arts teachers are best qualified to decide what constitutes informed practice and curriculum content; that NCTE urge legislative bodies and the agencies that regulate education to directly involve professional language arts organizations in the development of all legislation, regulations, and guidelines governing English language arts practice and curriculum; and that NCTE oppose the imposition by mandate of curriculum and practice that have not been developed with the involvement of professional language arts organizations and English language arts teachers.

Elements of Curriculum Development

Developing curriculum that prepares students to meet the Common Core State Standards in writing starts with understanding and analyzing the standards, as we did in Chapter 1. The next step is to understand the Common Core assessments, especially the writing performance tasks. We discuss these individually in Chapters 6 and 7, but it is important to get the "big picture."

Look at the Big Picture Before Backward Planning

Teachers who are developing curriculum for, say, the eleventh-grade year, can first take a look at the CCSS assessments for that year. This example is from the PARCC.

Grade 11 Summative Assessment
Performance-Based Component

Literary Analysis Task	*Narrative Task*	*Research Simulation Task*
The Literature Task plays an important role in honing students' ability to read complex text closely, a skill that research reveals as the most significant factor differentiating college-ready from non-college-ready readers. This task will ask students to carefully consider literature worthy of close study and compose an analytic essay.	The Narrative Task broadens the way in which students may use this type of writing. Narrative writing can be used to convey experiences or events, real or imaginary. In this task, students may be asked to write a story, detail a scientific process, write a historical account of important figures, or to describe an account of events, scenes, or objects, for example.	The Research Simulation Task is an assessment component worthy of student preparation because it asks students to exercise the career- and college-readiness skills of observation, deduction, and proper use and evaluation of evidence across text types. In this task, students will analyze an informational topic presented through several articles or multimedia stimuli, the first text being an anchor text that introduces the topic. Students will engage with the texts by answering a series of questions and synthesizing information from multiple sources in order to write two analytic essays.

End-of-Year Assessment

On the end-of-year assessment, students have the opportunity to demonstrate their ability to read and comprehend complex informational and literary texts. Questions will be sequenced in a way that they will draw students into deeper encounters with the texts and will result in more thorough comprehension of the concepts, as the sample items found at this PARCC website show. You can access these items in our online resources.

(http://www.parcconline.org/samples/english-language-artsliteracy/grade-11-elaliteracy)

Backward Planning

We believe in the "backward planning" approach to unit planning and curriculum development; this means looking at the final performance assessments in writing, above. However, there are other things to consider. When we work with a school district to develop curriculum, we also invite first-year writing instructors from the local university to talk with us about local expectations (recognizing that not all students will be in these specific classes). Often the WPA (Writing Program Administrator) of first-year writing can provide this perspective. In addition to listening to the writing requirements in first-year college writing classes, we also listen to local employers. Both colleges and employers value writing skills that are not easily measurable, such as creativity, audience awareness, adaptability, and innovative thinking. Curriculum planning needs to help students develop these skills as well.

Curriculum Mapping

Once teachers have a clear sense of the outcomes for the grade level, they can work backward, mapping out what standards and skills will be addressed when, breaking up the year into units of study. They can ask questions like these:

- How do we know whether students are progressing towards mastery of the standards?
- Which standards should be mastered and at which part of the year?
- Are all standards addressed in the units?
- How will student performance be assessed at the end of each unit?

During the mapping process, teachers can determine whether and where their units have gaps and overlaps. Is there repetition where it doesn't need to be? Were any standards missed? At this point, teachers analyze the sequence of the units, making sure the order of the units allows students to build on skills as they move through the school year. Once all the standards are mapped out, teachers can plan backward within each unit by describing what kind of student performance would indicate standards mastery at the end of the unit. Teachers often have very different ideas about what a final assessment would look like, which is why it is so important for this work to be done collaboratively and with consensus-building processes in place.

Unit Development

Once unit assessments are in place, teachers can plan learning activities that will help students get there. This can be done individually—teachers are all trained in and have experience with developing units. There are many different paths to the same learning outcome, so there is no need to dictate a single approach. New teachers may appreciate access to units that are further developed, however, with a range of learning activities, teaching materials, and resources to choose from.

Unit Assessment

Another element of curriculum development that benefits from a collaborative approach is deciding what evidence will show that students have met the standards. For this, teachers should come together and examine real student work using a common rubric. Teachers will need to come to consensus on work samples that show mastery. Once these are agreed upon, teachers can revisit the learning activities and align them more closely with the standards and unit assessment.

Professional Development

Going through the process of curriculum development collaboratively can raise awareness of what teachers know and don't know. When we have worked with groups of teachers on curriculum development, the work has often spawned a professional development "wish list." It is desirable for districts to provide this professional development so that each and every teacher can implement the new curriculum successfully.

New Impacts on Curricula

The Common Core State Standards have an impact on curriculum development that previous educational reform did not. For example, now that there are Common Core State Standards in writing for history, science, and technical subjects, the teaching of writing is no longer solely in the curriculum of the English teacher. Because the writers of the Common Core define "technical subjects" as pretty much all other content areas, this means that, for the first time, teachers across the content areas have some common goals and common concerns. What does this mean for curriculum planning? Well, in the past teachers needed only to plan in their own content area. Now, it makes sense to collaborate across subject areas to make sure students are meeting the writing standards.

The other feature of the CCSS that will affect curriculum planning is that students will read increasingly complex texts. For teachers whose students are currently not reading at grade level, it will be especially challenging, as much differentiation of instruction will be needed to make sure those students make gains instead of falling further behind. Another consequence of this feature is that English teachers may need to readjust their cherished reading lists to make sure students are reading increasingly complex texts from grade to grade. Curriculum planning groups will need to meet in vertical teams to look at the texts read from grade to grade.

One Important Global Curriculum Change You Can Make on Your Own

Although a collaborative process of curriculum mapping and creating CCSS units using "backwards design" is ideal, this process takes time and not all teachers will have opportunities to work together. There is, however, one global change teachers can make to their own curriculum to improve student writing, and that is to simply increase the amount of writing that students do.

Sometimes teachers, especially English language arts teachers, resist assigning more writing because they perceive this will increase their already heavy workload of papers to grade. Content area teachers may resist having their students write because they don't know how to grade writing. Although she later changed her view, one seventh-grade reading teacher said, "I don't mind writing, but I hate to grade writing. Therefore, I don't assign much writing. Because I am a perfectionist, and if a student misses a comma or a period, it just eats me."

Solving this problem means thinking differently about the kinds of writing students do. For Kelly, this "ah-ha" moment came when she encountered "Levels of Writing" in Rhoda Maxwell's *Writing Across the Curriculum* (1995). Level 1 writing is personal, informal, and ungraded; Level 2 writing is for an audience, more formal, and graded; and Level 3 writing is public, formal, and high stakes. Writing on demand for the CCSS performance tasks is Level 3 writing, but that does not mean that students should be doing only Level 3 writing to get better at it. Writing skills are best developed at Levels 1 and 2. Levels of writing are applicable to any content area. Thinking about the writing assigned and graded in terms of these levels helps teachers keep a healthy balance of writing assigned.

The levels are akin to the food pyramid. The majority of "healthy" writing should be at Level 1. This is really where writing fluency is developed and where writing-to-learn takes place. Level 3 writing should be as rare as desserts. Career-ready writers need to be proficient in Level 3 writing given that the quality of their letters, emails, proposals, reports, and presentations will have a big influence on their reputation and even promotion.

Figure 3.1 shows a basic definition of Maxwell's "Levels of Writing" framed in terms of RAFT+ E (Role, Audience, Format, Topic, plus Evaluation):

Online 3.2
Maxwell's Levels of Writing

Figure 3.1 Maxwell's Levels of Writing

	Level 1 Writing	Level 2 Writing	Level 3 Writing
Role	Casual self, informal	Public self, slightly less informal	Professional self, formal
Audience	Self, close friends, peer group in class	All to the left, plus teacher, parents, other adults	All to the left, plus audience outside the classroom, one that may judge the work for another purpose such as to decide on a scholarship, job, or promotion
Format	Journal, notes, prewriting (such as, lists, maps, outlines, mapping, freewriting), rough drafts, etc.	Homework, chapter tests, revised drafts, reports, etc.	Final drafts, researched reports, letters, proposals, etc.
Topic	History: Free write everything you know about slavery.	History: Write a report about the events leading up to the abolishment of slavery.	History: Construct a coherent essay that integrates your interpretation of Documents A–I and your knowledge of the period referred to in the question. 1. Analyze the international and domestic challenges the United States faced between 1968 and 1974, and evaluate how President Richard Nixon's administration responded to them (2011 AP US History Exam).

(continues)

Figure 3.1 Maxwell's Levels of Writing *(continued)*

	Level 1 Writing	Level 2 Writing	Level 3 Writing
Topic	Science: List the parts of a cell.	Science: Read a current science article and then write a 3-paragraph "Issues, Evidence, and You" essay (from Marc Siciliano in Daviss and Thier's *The New Science Literacy*, pp. 70–71).	Science: Lab report
	English: Highlight all the references to blood in the first act of *Macbeth*, then free write on what you think blood symbolizes (from O'Brien's *Shakespeare Set Free*).	English: Decide on an interpretation of a particular scene of *Macbeth* and then "pitch" your idea to your acting group.	English: Perform your scene in Macbeth and have a member of your company explain your group's choices in setting, costume, and blocking.
Evaluation	Not graded, or graded only on completion or content	Limited or focused grading, such as grading for understanding of information	High-stakes grading—content and form are equally important; must be error free or close to it.

Classroom Moves: Level 1 Writing Activities in Math

Teachers of any subject who want to increase the amount of writing in their classes can use the list that follows to develop classroom materials. For example, what follows are some Level 1 writing prompts developed by math teachers for dealing with the concept of "order of operations."

Before Reading

- Write about what comes to mind when you hear "order of operations."

- Explain how to make cookies or another dish using a recipe.

- Describe a time when you went out to eat.

- What kinds of grouping symbols do you commonly use?

- What do you want to know about _____? (Choose one of the vocabulary words from this chapter.)

- What do you think the letters PEMDAS stand for?

- Make up words for PEMDAS that relate to your life.[1]

- What kind of information do you need to solve a problem?

- Write about something life changing. (Later, when introducing the negative sign before a parenthesis, make a connection with this quick-write: "This negative sign changes everything.")

During Reading

- Write a word problem that would require more than one "operation."

- Explain how you solve this problem. (Choose one from the middle of the chapter.)

- Give an example in which the order of operations needs to be used.

- How does the order of operations work differently from reading?

- What is the trickiest part of using the order of operations?

After Reading (Exit Slip)

- Create your own mnemonic device for remembering the order of operations.

---

[1] PEMDAS stands for Parentheses first, Exponents, Multiplication and Division, Addition and Subtraction. It refers to the order of operations for solving an equation.

- What do you struggle with when it comes to order of operations?
- Do we really need to have an order of operations? Why or why not?
- Solve one order of operations problem before leaving (the teacher separates them into correct and incorrect piles to help determine what needs to be taught at the next class).
- Create a jingle (poem, limerick, etc.) to remember what you learned about the order of operations.

These ideas show how Maxwell's "Levels of Writing" provides a useful heuristic for guiding a quick incorporation of writing practice into content area classrooms.

PLC ACTIVITY: LEVELS OF WRITING

In your professional learning community, brainstorm Level 1 writing activities for one of the units of study you have developed. Discuss how the writing activities can both help students increase the amount of writing they do and learn content material. Remember that Level 1 writing is ungraded.

As a follow-up activity, brainstorm Level 2 writing activities. Discuss how these activities can be assessed. Come back together after teachers have had a chance to try out one of the activities. Bring student samples and assess a few together. What can these work samples show about student strengths and weaknesses as writers? How do these findings affect future teaching decisions?

Lesson-Level Curriculum Changes

Another dimension of curriculum development occurs at the level of individual lessons. Here, for example, is a tenth-grade English lesson created by Lisa Fricke, under the direction of cooperating teacher Charles Lang, to address new Common Core standards dealing with interpreting information in diverse media and formats.

Informational Text Direction Styles
Common Core Standards

- Journal Entry (RI 9–10.3, W 9–10.10, SL 9–10.2)
- Station One: Textual Directions (RI 9–10.6)
- Station Two: Visual & Textual Directions (RI 9–10.3 SL 9–10.1)
- Station Three: Video & Audio Directions (RI 9–10.3 SL 9–10.1)

Learning Objectives

- Students will learn to follow step-by-step directions.
- Students will be able to evaluate directions.
- Students will be able to make recommendations to better the directions.
- Students will gain knowledge of basic origami.
- Students will increase their math awareness.
- Students will increase their motor skills.

Assessment

Formative Assessment: Journal entries will be graded based on reflection of the stations given. The students will answer what their strengths and weaknesses are with each type of directions and write what would have made each station easier.

   Formative Assessment: The two pieces of origami and the picture that is drawn will be graded on completion.

Rationale

This lesson allows the teacher to evaluate how each student responds to different types of instruction. In this lesson students will be given different examples of informational text, which will help them with creating their own instructional text in the future. There will be three stations, each with a different kind of informational text.

Activities

Journal Entry to Be Completed After Each Station

Directions: Reflect on the effectiveness of each station's directions.

- What was easy about each station?

- What was hard about each station?

- Is there anything that could be improved in each station?

- How would you make those improvements?

- Which station's directions did you prefer and why?

Station One: Textual—5 minutes

Directions: Complete the directions at your given substation by creating the object described.

Station Two: Text and Images—20 minutes

Directions: Complete the directions at your given substation.

- Origami Yoda Head

  - Allow students to struggle and to help one another as much as needed.

Station Three: Video and Audio—20–30 minutes

Directions: Complete the directions at your given substation by creating the object described.

- Origami Bird/Flower

  - Allow students to struggle and to help one another as much as needed.

Materials

Station One: Students are to follow audio directions to draw an object.

Here are some simple directions that could be used:

http://www.wisc-online.com/objects/ViewObject.aspx?ID=CCS4007

Station Two: Students are to follow print directions for an Origami Yoda.

Designed and diagrammed by Marcela Brina, available at

http://www.artisbellus.com

Station Three: Students follow audio and video directions to create an origami bird.

Use the following YouTube videos or something similar:

Daily origami: Easy bird by happypuppytruffles

http://www.youtube.com/watch?v=Us99JPGG42g

OR for an easier version

See the origami flower by Yanghaiving

> http://www.youtube.com/watch?v=JTMJUNBA0es

Online 3.3
*Informational
Text Direction
Styles Lesson*

When Ms. Fricke reflected on this lesson, she was pleased with how it challenged students' cognitive skills. They had to complete the task without the easiest directions. It tested their patience and ability to follow directions. Ms. Fricke wrote, "They had to interpret what the directions were saying, and in the video session they had to be able to understand what the demonstrator was trying to get them to do. They also had to write a reflection on their frustrations and triumphs during the sessions." These are important skills for taking the new CCSS assessments online because students will have to deal with a lot of online directions before they even get to the test questions. This lesson could be adapted to different content areas as well. Nearly every content area includes informational text such as directions. For example, students could evaluate written, video, and oral safety directions in a shop class.

Processes That Support Lesson and Unit Development

Units and lessons are the visible products of curriculum development, but a number of processes support the development of lessons and units. Teachers need to continually evaluate as they proceed, assuring that the materials produced address local mandates as well as the more global issues raised by standards like the CCSS. Ideally these processes can be carried out collaboratively, with groups of experienced teachers working together, perhaps even with pre-service teachers. Even when regular face-to-face collaboration is not possible, teachers can share ideas online, as we explain next.

Checking for Text Complexity

Teachers who aim to prepare students for CCSS assessments may want to begin the process of curriculum development by considering the level of text complexity in the materials they plan to use. Figure 3.2 demonstrates how one group of teachers, led by Alissa Helm, analyzed a text they planned to use.

Although the reading level of this text was low, ultimately it was a good choice for the majority of students to read—it was accessible to all students, and teachers could supplement the reading with students having individual reading at their own levels through

Figure 3.2 Analysis of the Text Complexity of *Roll of Thunder, Hear My Cry* by Mildred Taylor

Qualitative Measures	Quantitative Measures
Structure	5.4 grade level according to Flesch Kincaid
Narrative, short, varied paragraphs with short or compound sentences; chronological order; no graphics; first-person narrator is the protagonist; includes dialogue.	5.7 grade level according to Scholastic 720–920 lexile Ages 9, 10, 11
Language Conventionality and Clarity	
African American dialect, slang. Few challenging vocabulary words. Conversational tone. Dialect and diction are easy.	
Knowledge Demands	**Reader-Task Considerations**
Historical: Great Depression and the economy, 1930s, Civil War, reconstruction, land issues. *Cultural:* African American culture, racism, poverty as life experience, regional knowledge—Mississippi, the American South, Southern dialect, discrimination, oppression. *Specialized terms:* Taxes, mortgage, sharecropping, KKK. *Other:* Family life and relationships, adult careers, author biography—critical lens. How the background topics look through a child's eyes; variations from today's language; representation of poverty in book versus today.	Cultural diversity of the class reading the book. Historical knowledge. Reading levels of students, ZPD. For students below grade level, what should be done? Consider how motivated students might be to read this book. What have students studied in history about this time and place?
Purpose	**Recommended Placement**
Multiple themes, some explicit, others implicit. New perspectives, social conflicts, historical fiction, read for enjoyment, what it was like to be black during this time period.	CCSS 6–8 text complexity band, although four pre-service teachers thought this novel should be placed in the elementary grades.

zone reading and supplementary texts. Also, students who had scored higher on the fall reading test read a more challenging book by the same author that dealt with many of the same themes and issues—*The Land* by Mildred Taylor.

Big Idea, Enduring Understandings, and Essential Questions of the Unit

Another process underlying the development of units and lessons is considering the big ideas, enduring understandings, and essential questions of the unit. This means thinking about the larger implications of what students are studying as well as what teachers want them to take away from the unit and the individual lessons within it. Here, for example, is how a group of seventh-grade teachers addressed this aspect of curriculum development.

Big Idea: By understanding human nature, seventh graders question equity and justice in the past and present so that they can take a stand to foster and promote acceptance of others.

Enduring Understandings:

1. There are many types of people.

2. Reading isn't meant to paint the world perfectly; however, it exposes readers to the good and bad of human nature.

3. Reading is entertainment.

4. Novels allow readers to understand the past and present.

5. Using vocal expression when reading out loud makes understanding the content much easier to recognize.

6. Technology is a resource that can be used to find a deeper interpretation of the content.

7. Vocabulary, definitions, and roots are essential to understand all types of reading.

8. Authors use a variety of different literary devices to develop the ideas, events, and characters in the novel.

9. Applying a close reading to all types of texts is important for understanding.

Essential Questions:

1. What can we learn about today's real-world problems based on challenges from the past?

2. How does understanding problems from the past impact our actions of today?

3. Is fair always equal?

4. What does family mean to the different characters in the novels?

5. What is racism and where do we see it in today's world?

6. Why should we read ROTHMC and/or *The Land*?

7. What is the theme in ROTHMC and/or *The Land*?

8. In what time period do the novels take place and why does it matter?

Alignment with Standards

Another important step in curriculum development is evaluation of what has been produced. Will the unit and the lessons within it help students reach the expected levels of proficiency? One way to do this is to consider which standards have been addressed. For example, here is how the teachers who developed the ROTHMC unit evaluated it in terms of the CCSS RL.1: "Cite several pieces of textual evidence to support analysis of what the text says explicitly as well as inferences drawn from the text." They provided these evidence statements: (1) Students have completed activities where they defend claims from the book with textual evidence, and have identified patterns of behavior in specific scenes. (2) Final test assessment asks students to draw inferences from quotes. Other standards for this unit were RL 7.3, RL 7.4, RL 7.6, RL 7.7, RL 7.9, W 7.2, W 7.3a & d, W 7.6, W 7.9, SL 7.1, L 7.4a–d, L 7.5a–c, and L 7.6.

Another way to evaluate units and lessons is to look at them in light of NCTE standards.

These examples show how teachers working on the ROTHMC unit used these standards.

1. NCTE Standard #1:

> Students read a wide range of print and nonprint texts *to build an understanding of texts, of themselves, and of the cultures of the U.S. and the world;* to acquire new information; to respond to the needs and demands of society and the workplace; and for personal fulfillment. Among these texts are fiction and nonfiction, classic and contemporary works.

> *Rationale: To address the italicized part of the standard above, we will have students read letters from children to the president during the Great Depression, read about the conditions of the people during the Great Depression, watch*

a video clip on "sit-ins" during the Civil Rights movement and a video on the historical context and adversity during the Great Depression. The essay (and possibly short answer) part of the test will assess their understandings of how ROTHMC relates to the other texts they've studied. The status updates student write on the web pages will provide a means for assessing student performance on this standard.

2. NCTE Standard #9:

Students develop an understanding of and respect for diversity in language use, patterns, and dialects across cultures, ethnic groups, geographic regions, and social roles.

Rationale: Throughout the unit, students will be learning about the historical context of ROTHMC, and will be drawing parallels between events that occur in the text and real historical events. By reading about the family of ROTHMC, students will gain an understanding of their background. Along with the book, students will also read primary documents that give context to that period in American history. Students will learn about the specific language use and dialect in the historical context of the book. This standard will be assessed through students' writing from the perspective of a character.

Other NCTE standards addressed by the unit were numbers 2, 3, 8, and 12.

With the big idea, enduring understandings, and essential questions established by the curriculum committee (with input from all teachers at the grade level), teachers could move to design individual lessons. What follows is a sample lesson from this unit.

Roll of Thunder, Hear My Cry Lesson Plan: Seventh-Grade Language Arts

85-minute class period

Objectives

- Students will read and analyze information pertaining to the portrayal of racism in today's society.

- Students will compare and contrast racial issues from the novel *Roll of Thunder, Hear My Cry* with racial issues present in today's society.
- Students will collaborate in groups and participate in a written discussion about racial issues.

Materials/Resources

- A copy of the article "Black + White Proms" written by Jessica Press for each student
- Racism: Then vs. Now worksheet
- Pencil/Paper

Activities

Bell Ringer: Upon entering the classroom, students will respond to the following prompt in their writing journals: Do you think that racism is present in today's society? If yes, give examples. If no, explain why you believe this.

Zone Reading: Allow students to find a comfortable spot in the room and let them read silently a book of their choice.

Kinesthetic Activity: Where Do You Stand?

- Ask students to take a stand on racism. Assign one wall of the room as "Yes, racism is still a big issue in America" and the other wall as "No, there isn't racism in America anymore." Ask students to recall their response from the bell ringer and, based on that answer, choose a side and stand by that wall.
- Ask several students to share their reasons for their choice.

Whole-Class Reading

- Pass out a copy of the article to each student and instruct the class to do a quick preread of the article.
  - Look at pictures, captions, headings, and diagrams.
  - Ask students to share what their predictions are for this article.

- As a class, read the article together. The teacher will begin by reading the first page and then use the popcorn strategy to have students read the remainder of the article.

Written Discussion

- Count students off into groups of four and have each student take out a sheet of paper.
- Give students directions for the activity.
  - Rather than having a verbal discussion about this article, students will have a written discussion.
  - They will begin by doing a free write for two minutes (make sure they write for the entire time) about their reaction to the article. Give them the following ideas for starting their freewrite:
    - What did you think about while reading this?
    - What reactions, thoughts, questions, or feelings do you have about the article or this topic?
    - Remind students to keep their pen to their paper and not to worry about spelling or grammar, just get their ideas down. Also remind them to use neat handwriting since they will be passing their papers.
  - After two minutes, instruct students to pass their papers to the person sitting to the left in their group and read what is written on the paper. Students will then write a response, question, comment, or connection to what is already written on the paper. Students should write their names after their response.
    - Instruct students to write as if they are having a conversation with the person.
    - Allow students enough time write down several sentences. Remind students to continue writing until the time is up.
  - Pass the papers until they come back to the original owner.
- *Group Activity:* Hand out the compare/contrast worksheet to students and allow them to work with their groups to complete the worksheet.
  - Ask students to think about the similarities and differences between this article and the racism shown in *Roll of Thunder, Hear My Cry*.

- Have a brief discussion comparing/contrasting the article and novel to get students thinking about the questions on the worksheet.

Assessments

- Students will hand in their written discussion sheets and be given points for participation in the activity. This will be an informal formative assessment of the student's understanding of the article.

- Students will turn in their "Racism: Then vs. Now" worksheet at the end of the class period. This will be a formative assessment worth 25 points. Students will be graded on completion, their ability to follow directions, and the extent of their ideas.

Online 3.4
Racism in Roll of Thunder, Hear My Cry *and in Today's World*

Figure 3.3 Racism in *Roll of Thunder, Hear My Cry* and in Today's World

Name: _____

Section 1: In your groups, discuss and write down how racial issues have changed since the time period of *Roll of Thunder, Hear My Cry* and how they have stayed the same.

	Similarities	Differences
List some of the similarities and differences in racism from the time period that *Roll of Thunder, Hear My Cry* was set (1933) and the time period the article "Black + White Prom" was written (today).		

Section 2: Answer the following questions on your own. For each question, write a 2–3 sentence response. Remember to write in complete sentences.

1. Give an example of how you have seen racism in today's society.
2. Do you think enough change in racist behavior has taken place since 1933, the time in which *Roll of Thunder, Hear My Cry* was set?
3. What do you think can be done to make more of a change to eliminate all racism?

This combination of NCTE standards that support diversity and comprehension of texts, selves, and U.S. cultures with the CCSS emphasis on informational texts can enhance student learning. A unit like this can lead students to make thoughtful connections between texts and demonstrate new insight into key themes.

Resources to Support Curriculum Development

Whether you are working on curriculum development by yourself or participating in a collaborative project, it is inevitable that you will, at some point, start looking for resources. You will want to learn more about what other teachers have done, how they have answered the questions that are nagging you, or what materials they are using in teaching a given topic. The good news is that the CCSS has generated a proliferation of resources, but the bad news is that it is not always easy to sift through everything effectively. Fortunately, there are groups that have done this sifting.

Literacy in Learning Exchange

Professional associations have undertaken leadership in identifying useful resources for teachers. The National Council of Teachers of English (NCTE) has joined a number of other professional organizations, including the National Council of Teachers of Mathematics (NCTM), National Council for the Social Studies (NCSS), and National Science Teachers Association (NSTA) in an online resource for all teachers—the Literacy in Learning Exchange. This resource is hosted by the National Center for Literacy Education (NCLE). You can set up a free account at http://www.ncte.org/ncle, which will give you access to an easily searchable site, the ability to create and follow groups working on the same issues you are working on, and the ability to comment on and generally engage socially with other teachers in your discipline who are creating Common Core standards-based resources.

For example, if you are a social studies teacher working on curriculum, you can "follow" a group like the, Social Sciences Assessment, Curriculum, Instruction (SSACI), a working association of educators interested in implementation of Common Core Standards related to social studies instruction and the new College, Career, and Civic Life (C3) Framework for Social Studies. If you are wondering how to attend to professional development alongside writing CCSS-aligned curriculum, you can read articles like "Creating a

Culture of Teacher Learning: Thinking about the Common Core Standards Systemically"
by Kailonnie Dunsmore.

The National Writing Project

NWP's mission is to improve the teaching of writing, K–16. Its model of teacher development is a grassroots one: the most talented K–16 teachers (in all subject areas) attend a four-week summer institute in which they refine their best practices for teaching writing, investigate current research on writing instruction, and develop workshops for other teachers. Through local in-service and continuity programs, these teachers share the knowledge they gain with a wider audience of educators.

At the NWP site, http://www.nwp.org/, you will find dozens of articles and books about other teachers who have undertaken curriculum development. Your local writing project site may also be a resource in providing professional development to deal with the CCSS.

The main thing to remember with writing or revising curriculum to prepare students for the assessments that accompany the Common Core State Standards is that you are not alone. Teachers all over the country are working with the same issues, and we can learn from each other. Finally, don't pile on more, more, more! With each new thing you add to your curriculum, take something away that is not working or not research based, or that is more about you than your students. Be honest and courageous, like the seventh-grade teacher who let go of her own obsession with correctness to allow her students more time to practice Level 1 writing.

Chapter Four

Processes of Writing on Demand

CHAPTER OVERVIEW *This chapter provides strategies for:*

- *adapting the processes of writing to both the classroom (writing to construct knowledge) and the testing environment*

- *showing how invention, or prewriting, strategies can be varied and helpful in building writing fluency*

- *making drafting recursive*

- *re-visioning a piece of writing*

- *eliciting effective peer response*

- *encouraging students to develop their metacognition and to transfer writing skills to other settings.*

Even though time is limited, successful student writers do have a process for writing on demand, or, rather, *processes* (because they each have their own processes). Using a writing process involves complex decision making, including finding a focus, deciding on an approach, determining priorities, and polishing the language. All students will take a different route through these decisions, but they will go through them. What teachers can do is help them on their individual journeys.

In a sincere effort to help struggling writers, teachers sometimes break down and simplify the writing process, providing so many supports along the way that when students face their first writing assessment independently, they flounder. Teaching students to write does not mean just teaching them how to create a certain kind of product (such as a lab report or essay), but teaching them how to develop their own processes, which involves deep and metacognitive thinking. Students need to learn to ask themselves questions

65

like these: "Will my audience understand this part?" "What can I do to make it more persuasive/informative/entertaining for its purpose?" "What *is* the purpose of this piece of writing?"

To initiate a conversation about writing process in your professional learning community, start by writing. Invite each person to do a quick-write describing her or his own writing process. All teachers write, so just pick the last piece you had to write—whether it was an email to parents, a proposal for a mini-grant, or a personal piece of writing—and think about the steps you took from start to finish.

After 10 to 15 minutes of writing, share with a partner or the group. We are predicting that no two people had the same process. In fact, if teachers were to compare their process for that piece of writing with their process for another piece, they might find that their process is different each time. Furthermore, the processes of adults are different from the processes of young people. In your PLC, share the kinds of process strategies that each of you has found works well for the grade level and subject you teach.

Owning one's writing process and knowing what questions to ask of one's writing is especially important for students who take the CCSS assessments. Teachers can't sit beside students during the test and tell them what kind of prewriting to do or how long to take doing it. Because fostering this kind of independence is so important, we assert that the processes of writing on demand can be learned within a larger, more robust engagement with a writing process that encourages student independence.

In fact, we would argue that it is *only* through teaching a robust and flexible writing process—then facilitating students' ownership of their process—that teachers can really prepare students for writing on demand.

Transfer: Internalizing One's Own Writing Process

Transfer is the ability to take knowledge learned about how to write in one situation, such as a secondary classroom, and carry it to another situation, such as a college classroom or a workplace. For writing transfer to take place, students need to be in charge of and to manipulate their own processes. This kind of preparation helps students transfer what they learn about writing in one class to many other situations, including assessment. When we interviewed students who had been successful at writing-on-demand tests, we found they both owned their individual strategies and could transfer these strategies from one situation to another. One of the most common strategies was to have a process for writing the essay on demand. We also found that these students could easily describe their thinking process as they completed the test. Here is how Swathi describes her prewriting phase when writing on demand:

> On the AP poetry question, I read through the question—looking at the question, it's important—and highlight the significant words, like compare and contrast, so I know what I need to be doing with the essay, then I read through the two poems, underlining what I think is important and making notes in the margin, then I go back to what I have written and quickly make a rough, rough outline. I use arrows to link ideas and then I just write. If there's time at the end, I do go back. I have to control myself to just fixing little things, because I'll hate the essay and try to rewrite the whole thing. I'll want to move big chunks of writing. The little things I fix are things that would annoy me when I'm reading it. If I forget a sentence, I would add it, sentences that would drive my point home or make my writing a bit sharper.

These students had individual processes—they had not been taught a "formula" for writing on demand. They had been exposed to an array of writing process strategies and adapted them for their own use. There were some common parts in their processes, however. The first part was to analyze the prompt and do some prewriting, which took about 5 minutes (out of the 30 minutes they had to perform the task). The second part was quick drafting, about 20 minutes, and the third part was to revise. This included anything—from adding sentences to clarify the argument, to changing words to eliminate repetitions or get at a more precise meaning, to using arrows to indicate a different order of paragraphs. Students spent 3 to 4 minutes on this kind of revision, and the final minute was devoted to editing.

We asked these students to share advice for other students facing the same task. Here is what Maya had to say:

> My number one piece of advice for students taking a writing test is to prewrite—it doesn't have to be long—even 2 to 3 minutes. When I was an amateur, I would just pummel my way through a timed essay, but now I just

take some time to compose my thoughts, and it helps me connect things better.

Another successful test-taker, David, suggested this on-demand writing process:

Once you have your essay prompt, just try to calm down. If it's hard, just think for 5 to 10 minutes, even if you don't know anything about it, just think logically about what you think someone would say. Imagine what you are going to write about and just start writing. Keep writing. Don't spend too much time on your intro. It will come to you naturally. As you are writing your sentence, the next sentence will come to you. Just keep going.

In the next section we will go over the different strategies for the various stages of the writing process. But first we need to talk about the most important, yet largely invisible, part of the process—motivation.

Motivation and the Writing Process

Motivation is key when it comes to starting the writing process. For the process to become deep and meaningful, the writer has to be engaged. Just as readers improve fluency when they have time and space to read for pleasure, writers improve fluency when they have opportunities to write for themselves and for pleasure. This is called Level 1 writing (from Maxwell's "Levels of Writing," which we discussed in Chapter 3). Keep in mind that Level 1 writing should not be graded. Students need daily opportunities to do this kind of writing, which means they need to be writing in multiple classes—in science, in math, in history, in electives.

Another way to motivate students to write is to provide reasons for writing. Kelly Gallagher has done a great job of laying out strategies for this in his book *Teaching Adolescent Writers*. Here is what he tells students in his classroom:

1. WRITING is "hard," but hard is rewarding.
2. WRITING helps you sort things out.
3. WRITING helps persuade others.
4. WRITING helps to fight oppression.

5. WRITING makes you a better reader.

6. WRITING makes you smarter.

7. WRITING helps you get into and through college.

8. WRITING prepares you for the world of work.

Before starting a new writing project with students, have a "why" ready. If it is really difficult to motivate students to do the piece of writing, it might be worth thinking about how the assignment can be changed to make it authentic. In her professional writing class, Kelly Sassi found her students' letters of complaint lacked audience awareness. When Kelly made it real by requiring students to write a genuine complaint letter (those to cell phone companies seemed most popular) and send it to the company, she found students were more motivated to engage in the writing assignment. As part of the process, students examined mentor texts exemplifying effective features such as using a polite tone and making a specific request. Students reported back at the end of the semester to share the results of their complaint letters. One student got a coupon for a free pizza after complaining about poor service. Another actually did get a new cell phone. Sharing these stories of success with the next semester's class increased motivation further.

A Look at the Processes of Writing: Prewriting

Once students are motivated, the next step to successful writing is the generating of ideas, called *prewriting*, or *invention*. Attention to prewriting is important because, for many students, serious writing anxiety begins at the very onset: Looking at a blank page or computer screen can cause anxiety, and the longer one looks at it, the higher the anxiety. Although not all students need guidance or work with prewriting—for a lucky few, writing ideas seem to present themselves readily—most students will benefit from work with a variety of prewriting strategies.

Prewriting techniques are not only useful as the first step of a longer process, but they also can function as writing activities in and of themselves that help students build confidence and develop fluency. Probably the simplest and most versatile of these is freewriting.

Classroom Moves

Freewriting

Freewriting is a brief (3–5 minute) timed writing during which the writer puts pen to paper (or fingers to keyboard) and just writes, writes, writes. The topic, of course, is the focus, but even if writers find themselves writing the same word time and time again, or something such as "this is stupid—I don't know what to write," they keep writing. There is no stopping for the whole time. When using a computer, it can also be helpful to turn off the screen to avoid looking at the writing and getting hung up on editing or revising when the writing isn't fully developed. For some, this can be freeing.

Freewriting can, by its very physical act of continuing to write, generate ideas and fluency. It is an individual prewriting activity and, clearly, should be used selectively, at the beginning of writing or when students become stalled and are running out of ideas.

Freewriting can be used strategically to build fluency, one of the writing skills needed for on-demand writing tasks. Next you'll see some sample 10-minute freewrites written by a middle school student named David. Kelly knew David to be a competitive person, so she asked him to count the number of words in his 10-minute freewrite (see Figure 4.1) and then suggested he challenge himself to write more words each time. David rose to the challenge, as you can see in Figure 4.2.

Figure 4.1 Ten-Minute Draft

Ten-Minute Draft	David's Number of Words
#1	125
#2	154
#3	179

Figure 4.2 David's Ten-Minute Drafts

Ten-Minute Draft #1	Ten-Minute Draft #2	Ten-Minute Draft #3
To play with my gamecube, I press the power button and then these squares appear and then you start playing. In madden NFL 2005 I enjoy being the patroits and battle every other team. I like the half back named Cory Dillion and I make him the player of the game. The most points I made in a single game is 104. I creamed the other team. Another record I forced 4 interception 2 force fumbles and 12 sacks. It was totally awesome. Sometimes I can hold them so they can't even get seven points. Maybe a field goal but no touchdown. I always said to myself it takes about an hour but it only seems like 20 minutes. Time flys when I'm having fun.	If I could change the world, I would make sure there are no homeless people and no hobos looking for a job. I would make North Korea, South Korea, and America have peace. No terrorism, no fight, no wars, but peace. I would make it sports land by putting all the content together and call it sports land or electronic land so you either like sports or electronics or both. If you don't like ether, you must go to the top of the land called dumbo land. It's where you sit around doing nothing. In the sports field, you could play any sport in the world, or make up sports. In electronics they have a tournament to see who's the best at each game. There a hospital and you can go home and take a break and come out again. Everybody must go home when both places are closed. It would be so fun.	My school is school David and in the morning I take the bus and go to school. First I have gym. We play dodgeball and after we have some time too, so we play basketball. After I have snack, my snack is a chocolate chip cookie and some milk. After we go out for a break. We play shoe-flinging contest. I won because mine went 6 yards. Later we have lunch and mine is cottage inn pizza with pop. When we have lunch, recess we played four square. After in math we play math game like math baseball. For science we would watch a video. We have another recess except this time much longer, in fact a hour longer. After, we play around in our classroom. When the bell rings, we get our stuff and get on the bus. Since we were so good everybody got candy when they got off. Then I came home and play madden NFL 2005 and I win 63 to 0. No home work today so I go out and play with my . . .
125 words	154 words	179 words

David chose topics that were of interest to him at the time and pushed himself to write more fluently with each successive quick-write.

Listing

Listing is a quick and easy way of getting ideas. For more narrow writing topics (for example, characteristics of the medieval period, reasons to exercise, or animals one would expect to see in a particular habitat), listing can be focused and helpful, especially if the list can be put into categories (such as economic, political, and religious characteristics of the medieval period).

One variation is to list categories first, then stop and look them over. Teachers can model the writing process for students by talking aloud while reviewing a list of categories. Here are some questions to pose:

- Does one list seem stronger than the other?
- Are there one or two items that I would like to pursue?
- Are there any related words or phrases?
- Do I see any patterns?
- Is there something you have written that sparks a new idea?

Listing is a great way to jump-start writing. Students can list by themselves, using buddies in a small group, or the whole class can consider a single topic—like climate change—and list together. Listing is a great prewriting strategy, and it is also a good stand-alone strategy for writing to learn in content area classes.

For fun prompts, see the book *List Yourself: Listmaking as a Way to Self Discovery* by Ilene Segalove and Paul Bob Velick.

Visual Invention

Our students live in a multimodal world, and, for many of them, the best way to get into writing is to start with something visual. Teachers can project a picture, painting, design, web page, or sketch onto the wall and ask students to write what they see. This could also be done with something three-dimensional, like a model or object that is related to the subject matter to be studied.

Variations: In science class, show students a photograph of a biome they are about to study. Have them free write for 5–10 minutes, describing what they see in the photograph.

Instead of giving students a visual and then having them write words about it, ask them to create something visual first. For those who are more visual and artistic, doodles, triangles, arrows, circles, and shapes can help with planning and prewriting. This is a very individual kind of invention strategy, but for some it is effective and important. After a few minutes of drawing or sketching, students can write about their drawings.

The website *Storybird*, www.storybird.com, can be used to help students get started writing. They click and drag images into a storyboard and then write a narrative to accompany the images.

Cubing

If you can imagine a cube (or make one for yourself out of a six-sided box covered with colored paper), you can put a command on each side. Have students choose a topic and then have them write for no more than 3–5 minutes a side:

Online 4.1
*Pattern for
Making a Cube*

- Describe it.
- Compare it (to something else, your choice).
- Associate it (as above).
- Analyze it.
- Apply it.
- Argue for or against it.

After writing to each side of the cube, students are pretty amazed by how much they have written.

Variations: Provide students with a topic (democracy, momentum, dance—whatever relates to your content area) and then do the cubing. Let them work in pairs or groups.

Once students have experienced these strategies, when they turn to any kind of writing—whether in class or in an on-demand situation—they can call upon these techniques and, using the prompts as cues, find ideas for what they want to say.

The Heart of the Process of Writing: Drafting

Some invention strategies, like cubing, can lead right into a draft. Students have written so much in their prewriting that they feel they're on their way to producing a draft. It is important that teachers do not truncate their process by insisting that all students move through certain steps in unison. Here are some ideas for helping students move from prewriting to drafting.

Looping

Looping is a technique described by Peter Elbow, which involves writing in short, timed segments. After students have done a freewrite for 3–5 minutes on a topic, ask them to *reread what they have just written* and look for a phrase, a word, or even a whole sentence that seems the most important: Elbow calls it the "center of gravity." Circle that word, phrase, or sentence and then start a second segment. Students should begin that segment by physically re-copying the circled segment, and continue to write for 3–5 minutes. Stop and repeat the process.

This activity can help students explore the differing ramifications of a topic. No more than about three segments, by the way, are truly helpful—students will probably tire of looping if they do it for much longer. One variation is to hand the first quick-write over to a peer and let the peer underline the most intriguing sentence.

Change of Perspective

Another way of moving from prewriting to draft is to have students read over what they have written and pretend to be someone who disagrees with their perspective. For example, if, when given the topic of climate change, the student wrote that he or she does not think it is happening, invite the student to take another point of view and write from that perspective.

Variation: After having students write about an issue, ask them to them explore multiple perspectives. For example, Kelly uses the issue of book banning. After students have done an initial freewrite, she hands out cards for role-playing. Students have to take on the role of the person on the card and write from that person's perspective. For book banning, cards include roles such as librarian, author, school board president, principal, English teacher, conservative parent, liberal parent, publisher, and so forth. Students can then trade cards and write again, or they can share what they wrote in small groups. A next step might be to have students think of their favorite book and write a letter to the newspaper arguing that the book should not be banned, making appeals to some of the different perspectives they have just explored.

Peer-Assisted Drafting

Most good writers call on the help of others to move drafts forward. "Can you take a look at this?" is a common question asked by those who write regularly. Tapping into the power of the peer can be specifically taught. We already mentioned how a peer can be used to move looping forward. Here are some other ideas:

- Give students time to read through each other's rough drafts. The reader should write three seed questions on the draft. A seed question is one that will grow—grow more text, that is. Here is an example of a seed question: What happens between the moment your main character realizes there is a problem and the big collapse of his world? This is *not* a seed question: I like your use of this word.

- Ask a partner to circle his or her favorite sentences. Enjoy the boost of confidence. Write more, trying to create more of what your partner liked.

- For a longer, messy draft, the partner can list the three most important points in the draft. This can help the writer see what is coming across to the audience and what is not. It can also help the writer decide what to keep and what to delete.

- Reverse outline: Ask a peer to write a subtitle for each paragraph of a draft. The writer can think about these questions: Is this what I expected? Have I given more attention to some ideas and not enough to others?

A Note About Drafting When Writing on Demand

Every student will have his or her own drafting patterns, and allowing students to claim this kind of individuality can be important. With on-demand writing, however, it will be necessary for students to do something more focused and even deliberate, and they need to know that the recursive aspect of drafting, while a normal and acceptable part of writing, must be compressed quite a bit in a timed situation. We discuss this further in Chapter 8.

Drafting may be different in class assignments than in a testing situation; however, when students are familiar and comfortable with their individual drafting habits and patterns, they will be far better equipped to write something extensive and focused in a testing environment. Drafting will be an exercise muscle that is strong and that can be used, if not effortlessly, at least consistently in any writing situation. When students understand their own drafting habits, they will be far better prepared for the pressures of writing on demand.

And one of the best ways to help students with drafting is a strong emphasis on invention. If students are comfortable getting ideas at the beginning and generating more ideas during their drafting, they are more likely to write quickly and to continue to write.

Improving the Writing: Revision, Editing, and Proofreading

Most students confuse the three activities of revision, editing, and proofreading. They are not interchangeable but are markedly different and represent very different levels of activity during the final draft of writing. Many students believe that the alteration of a single word, or the correction of capitalization and punctuation, is revision, but such is not the case. Students must look at the whole writing, not just at the word or sentence level. Revision is the major work of changing writing; editing and proofreading are last-stage polishing activities.

In general, *revision* is best thought of as re-vision, re-looking, re-working of a piece of writing. This may include changing significant portions of the writing, such as rearranging sections, deleting sections, rewriting openings and closings, adding new information, or even refocusing the entire piece. Revision can transform a piece of writing.

High school teachers Pam Fisher and Nancy Devine created something they call "ABCD-E Text Generation and Revision Protocol" to help students both generate and revise a text. They provide a template with the letters ABCD-E listed down the left side of the paper. These are the prompts for the letters:

- A = Action
- B = Background (descriptions of settings, people, context; internal thoughts of main character[s])
- C = Continue action
- D = Dialog (Conversation between two or more people, monologue, internal monologue, comment from another character)
- E = Ending

The ABCD-E sequence may be repeated as many times as the writer wishes. The ending may take any format(s) of text—dialog, action, description, or a combination thereof—in any order. In our online materials, you can find both the blank protocol form created by Nancy and Pam as part of their work co-directing the Red River Valley Writing Project Summer Institute and a model text that uses the protocol, titled "Found Dog."

Online 4.2
ABCD-E Protocol

Editing, on the other hand, is a look at a revised piece of writing to review and change word order, sentence structure, and to check usage issues. At this stage the major changes in the writing have been established; the changes made in editing are less intrusive and far less significant to the meaning of a final piece of writing.

Online 4.3
*Model Use of
ABCD-E Protocol:
"Found Dog"*

Proofreading is a last look at a revised, edited piece. It includes verification that all minor details of usage are addressed (such as capitalization, indentation of paragraphs, sufficient spaces between title and body, etc.). It is a final polishing.

Most students who find writing difficult from the onset resist revision and hope that proofreading and some minor editing will be all that is needed to improve their hard-won first draft. For most students, however, revision is the vital activity to learn and practice. One of the most powerful ways to encourage students to revise their work is to use peer-response writing groups; a section on establishing and maintaining those groups appears later in this chapter. Another powerful way to encourage revision is to model by doing it yourself. In *Write Beside Them*, Penny Kittle shows how to do this. She takes a rough draft and projects it so all can see. She then revises on the spot, talking aloud as she does so. Students are often relieved to see that their teacher's writing also goes through the messy process of revision.

On the other hand, there is also a real place for proofreading; many evaluators of writing tests cite inadequate proofreading as one thing they look for when considering the quality of writing samples. Although it is necessary to understand this last stage of correction in a broader context, proofreading is an important skill to use in writing-on-demand situations.

Teachers can help students make these distinctions by giving them drafts of papers and asking them to work with those drafts in different modes: revising, editing, and proofreading. If students can see and practice the difference between the major work of changing writing (revision) and the minor details of usage in proofreading (such as capitalization, indentation of paragraphs, sufficient spaces between title and body, etc.), they will be far better equipped to improve their own writing both in the classroom and in a testing environment.

Evaluation and Multiple Rubrics

Although publishing to a broad audience is often the end result of the process of writing, in writing on demand it is vital to remember that the audience is the evaluator. Accordingly, attention to specifics for writing assignments is vital, as evaluators will be looking specifically and consistently for certain qualities in the final writing product. How do we prepare students for this?

One crucial aspect of the process of writing is the use of evaluation and multiple rubrics. Giving students rubrics for their writing, or asking them to help create rubrics, will enable students to understand and participate in the evaluative process. When students prewrite, draft, and revise, they often are not clear about how a piece of writing might be judged, either by a teacher, a peer, or, in a testing situation, by the anonymous reader/grader. Students can, as part of their processes of writing, learn that certain rubrics and certain grading emphases will result in different evaluations of the very same paper, something few of them know. If, for instance, an assignment emphasizes voice, or organization, or narrative flair, the evaluative rubric should reflect that concentration. This kind of information is vital to students in their class writing and in a testing situation: Once students understand the range of evaluation, they have a better chance to write to specification, as well as to keep some of their individuality. For more information on this final step of the process of writing, evaluation, see Chapter 6.

As a last note, while evaluation of final drafts is expected and important to student writing improvement, grading rough drafts is not. To assign a value to a work in progress is counterproductive; as most teachers know, many things can happen between a promising rough draft and a final draft. A high grade on a draft can encourage students to stop working, and a low grade can so dishearten a student that he or she ceases to work. Giving students credit for drafting is certainly something we want to do in our classes, but grades on a draft, however tentative we intend them to be, are often seen by students as a final judgment.

Responding, Evaluating, and Grading

Whether we use just rubrics, just comments, or a combination, we give students feedback on their writing. There are different ways to react, and the distinction between responding, evaluating, and grading is important to note. The three activities are not necessarily mutually exclusive, but each differs somewhat from the others.

When we respond to students, we make an effort to talk to them, writer to writer. A teacher's response to a student paper should encompass three things:

1. *Personally link to something the student has written.* A teacher could write: "Yes: I had a similar experience; that would anger me, too. That happened to a friend of mine."

2. *Tell the student what a reader might like about what he or she has written.* The experience of reading the paper can be important: Pick one or two things the student does well and ask the student to think about them. A teacher could write: "Your introduction really grabs me—do you have any idea why that opening image is so powerful? You are using parallel construction effectively here—do you see how?"

3. *Ask the student questions about the draft, questions that suggest changes.* A teacher could write: "Look at your title—is that what this paper is really about? If not, what is it about? Can you find where you could break this long section into two paragraphs? What effect do you think this word has on what you are trying to say in this paragraph?" (Christenbury 2000)

When a teacher *evaluates* a paper, the emphasis should be on how well the paper is doing what it does, on how close the paper comes to what it is trying to do. This may mean more emphasis on #2 (above) and more direction on #3. For example, a teacher could make comments such as, "I am lost in this section—what is it about?" or "Your paragraphs are so long you are combining a number of points—can you break the section on page 2 into two or three paragraphs?" Evaluation can also be a situation in which one draft is specifically compared to another—how close does this version come to a model? Obviously, rubrics can be vital in evaluation, and teacher comments can accompany scores and percentages on a rubric.

To *grade* a paper requires a letter or numerical designation and some sort of final evaluative comment. As was noted, a rubric with percentages or points can help make this final grade explicit. Many rubrics use points and percentages that can be readily translated into grades. Further, those rubrics often indicate that mechanics and usage should not constitute fully half of the final grade but something far more reasonable, such as 10 or 20 percent.

Rubrics are constants in on-demand writing; when students are used to evaluative rubrics in classroom assignments, they will readily make the transition to the kind of evaluative requirements set out in on-demand writing.

Online 1.9
*Framework
for Success in
Postsecondary
Writing: Full
Document*

Notes on College Readiness

The authors of the "Framework for Success in Postsecondary Writing" remind us, "Writing processes are not linear. Successful writers use different processes that vary over time and depend on the particular task. For example, a writer may research a topic before drafting; then, after receiving feedback, conduct additional research as part of revising. Writers learn to move back and forth through different stages of writing, adapting those stages to the situation. This ability to employ flexible writing processes is important as students encounter different types of writing tasks that require them to work through the various stages independently to produce final, polished texts" (p. 12). You can find a link to the full document in the online resources.

RESEARCH AND POLITICAL CONSIDERATIONS

The following excerpt from an NCTE Research Policy brief titled "Writing Now" advocates a holistic approach to teaching writing and provides additional guidelines for thinking about what that means when it comes to writing process:

The holistic approach regards the "process model" of writing as flexible.

- Writing does not proceed in linear fashion from prewriting to drafting to revising. The revision practices of students become more effective when instructors help them to see that revision occurs at every stage of the writing process. Students benefit from a metacognitive understanding of revision; rather than just learning steps in a process, they should constantly reflect upon their own writing performances.

- Most teachers say they use a "process" approach to writing instruction, and students demonstrate familiarity with process tasks. However, research shows that the implementation of process approaches is flexible and varies from one classroom to another.

- Students who create high-quality writing plans, often involving reflection or awareness of their own thinking as well as personal goals for writing, produce stronger papers. Teachers can help students with this process by examining and responding to prewriting as well as drafts. When students

Online 4.4
Writing Now

are given explicit instructions in writing they can develop the ability to monitor and modify their own writing processes, and this, in turn, improves the quality of their writing. Such instruction can include strategies like goal setting and self-monitoring, which lead students to write longer, more developed, and qualitatively stronger texts (p. 4).

When it comes to writing on demand, it is not necessary to "teach to the test." Instead, students will benefit from being given many low-stakes opportunities to write to develop their fluency. These opportunities should be carefully designed to motivate students. Daily writing for pleasure is an excellent way to develop fluency. Metacognitive work should be included to help students recognize their individual writing process and transfer their learning about writing process strategies to their own writing process. Students who have a clear sense of their own process and are flexible enough to adapt it for different contexts will be able to contend with the writing on demand required by the new Common Core State Standards performance tasks.

Classroom Moves: The Process of Writing a "This I Believe" Essay

Eighth-grade teacher Dan Dooher has a unit on the "This I Believe" essay that has resulted in students who have a strong ownership of their writing process. In fact, some students work on creating new belief essays beyond the classroom unit.

First Lesson:

Quick write: List five to ten things you value, and note in a sentence or two after each one why you value them.

Drafting: Choose a couple of the things from your list that have a story to go with them. Begin telling that story.

Finding a purpose: Students listen to the purpose behind the "This I Believe" radio program. A link can be found here: http://www.youtube.com/watch?v=IgEOBJwWZ90.

Getting motivated: Listen to a pep talk. A link can be found here: http://www.youtube.com/watch?v=l-gQLqv9f4o

Drafting: Now that you're fired up, choose one of the stories related to something you value, and write or rewrite it.

Listening to and looking at models: Exemplar "This I Believe" essays are for students to listen to. Then students are given a hard copy of one work, and in groups they identify the parts of the model.

More drafting: Add to or revise your essay, using the structure your group identified.

During the first few lessons, Dan supplies multiple writing prompts to assist students in identifying their beliefs and provides a daily structure that helps students develop their drafts over time. Dan notes that students often discover their beliefs at different times via brainstorming lists of things they value or stories from their lives that have strong emotional meaning to them.

Structure:

Quick-write and discussion: Dan provides prompts at the beginning of the unit primarily to brainstorm content for the essay, while the prompts toward the end are used to discuss why or how students might do something to improve their draft.

Minilesson: Dan gives short lessons on essay structure and craft to help students revise and improve their drafts.

Mentor texts: Students listen to exemplar essays while following along with a copy of the essay. Next, they work in pairs or small groups, comparing lots of examples to help all students develop a better sense of the possibilities that lay before them.

Drafting: As students write, Dan holds individual conferences to help provide them with more specific feedback and individualized teaching. This part of the lesson is the longest, messiest, and most important for the development of student's essays.

Sharing: Dan provides time at the end of each lesson for students to share parts of their essays. This helps build community and ownership in the writing process.

Dan works with students individually throughout this process. The class is not working through these parts of the writing process in lockstep; the magic happens at different times for different students. Here are some sample student essays that his students have agreed to share. The students all had a different process for arriving at these final essays, and you will hear their individual voices.

I Believe Essay

by Ava

When I was in 3rd grade, I had a best friend. We were partners for every project and we sat by each other everyday during snack break. One day she walked up to me in the hall and told me I was dumb, mean, and that she didn't want to be my friend anymore. I cried for what felt like a week. I wasn't her friend after that, but I found out why she had said such mean things—she was being bullied for being friends with "the girl who wore weird clothes." I had a very hard time after that but soon things got better. I started talking to old friends, who now are some of my best friends, and making new friends. Before I knew it, I had stopped caring what the bullies thought of me and ignored them. That day, I gained something—self confidence.

I believe in the power of self confidence. After my experience, I only cared what my family and *true* friends thought of me. I ignored all of the negative things people said to and/or about me. Sure, I lost a friend but it doesn't bother me anymore. I have true friends that I know I can trust. I think self confidence moved me through this tough experience. I think people who have self confidence are able to move farther in life because they aren't afraid of what people think of them. Having confidence in yourself makes life easier and people who have confidence in themselves seem to be happier.

I have lost friends, I have gained friends, I have made hard decisions but I have moved on. Having confidence helps move you through life. Self confidence has a positive effect on everyone.

This I believe.

Labels are for jars, not people

by Elizabeth

I thank my doctor for telling me I have epilepsy. I believe that you should never label yourself until someone tells you. When you are so called "labeled," don't take it seriously or personal. Even though people do say "oh ya you're the girl with the seizures," and they usually laugh, or make fun of me, I just laugh too, because they are making fun of something I can't control. It's not like I pick a day to have a seizure because I'm thinking I'm not getting enough attention, it just happens and for how many seizures I have had, I get used to people asking questions.

Labels are for jars not people or in other words, don't label yourself. I'm the girl with epilepsy, but I am not the epileptic girl.

When I went to the doctor for the first time after having a seizure, they didn't officially say I had epilepsy or was epileptic, they said "We'll wait until you have another one so we can diagnose you." After 4 more seizures, I went to see a neurologist in Minneapolis, who specializes in teenagers with seizures. After a 5 hour doctor appointment, going thru every detail of all my seizures and 2 blood tests and an EKG, he told me "Elizabeth, you have epilepsy." In a way, I was really happy because I have waited for 3 years to be told I was epileptic. After the appointment I cried because I was finally given an answer, epilepsy.

Now I can inform people on my epilepsy and I'm not afraid to say it. I know that I have amazing friends who love me and are not scared of my seizures. I know that my friends are a little scared that I will have seizure, but I have trained them on what to do and they are always calm. What I am most thankful for is what my friends do to help me and that they don't define me as the epileptic one they treat me like me. The one thing about my seizures is that my mom was already informed about them because when you have a 1 pound 2 ounce baby they will probably going to have seizures so you should always keep that in mind.

Even though my doctor told me I had epilepsy, I take it as a compliment and not as an insult because I can't control them. It does not define me. However it helps to make me who I am and that is making me stronger. Yes, I will always have to live with seizures, but it's what I have not who I am. I believe you should not label yourself. Because being yourself is amazing. This I believe. Don't label yourself.

Dan Dooher had this to say about the student essay below: "I am very proud of Trystyn's essay. I think this project captured Trystyn's imagination. He put more care into his writing than he had earlier in the year, taking time to revise and share the essay with me prior to the due date! I especially loved how he came to realize that he enjoyed hard work because of the way it made him feel internally and not so much for the external rewards."

This I Believe

By Trystyn

This paper is about beliefs. My beliefs are that you should always be a hard worker. If you do that you'll get respect and people will have good memories about you. I'm going to tell you a story about a time I worked hard and tell you what happened in return.

One time I was at my grandma's and she needed help moving big rocks, also we had to break the rocks into pieces and even then they were still too heavy. To make the job easier; my grandma let me use the four-wheeler to move them. It still was hard work though it was during the summer so it was almost a hundred degrees. But I never stopped and I got the job done. My grandma saw how good I drove the 4-wheeler and now she lets me drive it for fun whenever I want. My grandma also told some friends about me and I got paid to crush cans. The neighbors also hired me to cut some firewood.

I like to work hard. The reason I like working hard is because I like the respect and the way I feel after all that hard work, the sense of accomplishment and sometimes the rewards that I get are awesome such as earning the 4-wheeler.

I think if everyone worked hard the world would be a lot better. There would be better grades, better technology, and people would be more respectful. Other people would be more respectful of other people's stuff because they know how hard they worked to get it.

Working hard is a good thing to believe in. The reason why is because when you work hard people respect you and some might even reward you. But I don't work hard for rewards, I work for that feeling I get when I finish something that took a lot of work. It's that sense of accomplishment that makes me believe in working hard.

This I Believe

by Hunter

I believe losing gives you wisdom. Making mistakes teaches you lessons. Losing lets you see the problems you faced, and what you need to overcome.

I don't remember the exact date, but I started to see him more often than the last time before, tell he was always there. His name was Johnny. He was my Mother's boyfriend. Me and him got along perfectly. I was like his son, and sometimes he'd call me his son.

As time went by him, me, my mom, and my brother were like a family. We were close. He was only guy that was like a father to me.

As time went on they got in fights. They didn't agree on stuff. People grow on each other then apart. My Mom and him broke up. But stayed friends.

Fast forward 2 or 3 years later. We're in the mall. My mom gets a call. She's crying more than I've seen before. It takes a while for me to find out but when I do I'm in shock. I didn't believe at first. I was in denial. The only man who was like a father dies. It took me a while to realize that I wasn't gonna see him ever again. Even after the ceremony I didn't cry. It took two years to realize it. The night I cried will be a night I don't think I'll forget in a while. Because I learned a lesson that night. That losing is a part of life, and everyone must feel it.

From that day on I started to live my life by not being afraid of losing. If I don't win a race in track, it doesn't affect me. If my team doesn't win a football game, I can accept it. It has given me wisdom, and with that wisdom I've realized that if you lose you can get back up. You can keep going, and carry on with life.

Having everything won't teach you a thing. Losing lets you see the flaws in the world. Losing is a part of life. This I believe is what losing means.

We believe that the rich writing process these students have engaged in will help them develop into writers for whom the new CCSS assessments are just one rhetorical situation with which they will be able to contend.

Chapter Five

Reading to Write on Demand

CHAPTER OVERVIEW *This chapter provides strategies for:*

- *motivating students to read for pleasure*

- *helping students read for information*

- *teaching students how to read for craft*

- *understanding subject area differences*

- *identifying rhetorical strategies*

- *accounting for language variation*

- *examining openings and closings.*

The Common Core State Standards (CCSS) emphasize the importance of writing in response to specific text(s), which means that students need to draw on textual evidence rather than simply state an opinion. Instead of writing about why school uniforms are/are not a good idea or whether the administration should have the right to search lockers, students are asked to read specified passages and draw support for their claims from these selections. Consequently, preparing students for CCSS assessments includes focusing on strategies for reading.

For some secondary school teachers, the idea of teaching reading seems alien. Didn't students learn to read in elementary school? Isn't high school the place where students use the reading skills they already have to gain important content knowledge? While it is true that high school students have learned a number of strategies for reading, they need to continue improving their skills, especially since each subject they study introduces new vocabulary, new concepts, new ways of expressing ideas, and new reading challenges. In the transition from elementary to secondary school, there is increased pressure on students to read in order to learn, and many students need explicit instruction in how to read effectively for this purpose. This chapter offers approaches to helping students become better readers in secondary school. A first step is for students to understand *why* they are reading; then they can turn to strategies for improving their reading.

Reasons for Reading

"Why do we have to do that?" is a common question in classrooms, and one worth answering. When students are asked to read a difficult text, or any text, they have a right to an explanation of why they should do it. Armed with an understanding of why they have to read, students are more motivated and more likely to do well. The following pages offer several reasons for reading and suggest ways of helping students become aware of them.

Reading for Pleasure

In the face of high-stakes tests and other pressures that position reading in terms of gathering information, of *doing* something, it is easy to forget that people also read because it can be a source of deep pleasure. If you ask students about their early experiences with reading, many will recall the delight of listening to books being read aloud, of escaping from their own spaces into other worlds, of responding emotionally to a story. The pleasures of reading have a place in preparing students for CCSS assessments because several of the pleasures of reading connect directly with skills that students will be asked to demonstrate.

The Pleasures of Language

Children's books and nursery rhymes demonstrate that even youngsters respond to the play of language. High school students learn terminology to describe forms of language play. Asking students to find words with sounds that resemble their meanings—that is, invoking the pleasures of onomatopoeia—is one way to help them (re)connect with the delights of language sounds. Read aloud a poem like Edgar Allan Poe's "The Bells" and encourage students to delight in the

> "tintinnabulation that so musically wells
> From the bells, bells, bells, bells,

Bells, bells, bells—
From the jingling and the tinkling of the bells."

In addition to fostering pleasure, attention to the sound of language can lead students to become better readers of other forms of language play, such as metaphor, alliteration, hyperbole, puns, and irony. Our students who listen to hip-hop and rap music already take pleasure in the sounds of language. Examples can be found at the Flocabulary website http://www.flocabulary.com/hiphopmetaphors/. Reading with attention to the sound in language can foster better reading of *tone*, which is important in many texts, including literary ones. Consider, for example, the opening line of *Romeo and Juliet*: "Two households, both alike in dignity…" Part of reading this Shakespearean play effectively is coming to understand the irony of this description of the Montagues and Capulets, who, in the course of the play, do a number of undignified things.

The Pleasure of the Unexpected

Reading involves prediction at several levels. In reading individual words, readers make millisecond predictions of what the first few letters will lead to. Will *wh* … lead to *whisper* or *whale*? In reading a sentence or short passage, readers think about what will come at the end, and in reading an entire text, readers try to figure out where it will go. One of the pleasures of reading mystery stories is trying to predict how they will end, and unexpected endings are part of that pleasure. One way to foster students' predictive abilities is to ask them to predict what will happen in a text before they read it.

Tasha Rios, an English teacher, did this on the day she handed out copies of Lorraine Hansberry's play, *A Raisin in the Sun*. Tasha had looked at a PARCC assessment that asked students to finish a story, and she decided that she could prepare her students for this kind of writing by requiring a related kind of prediction. After explaining the features of a play script, she told students they could read the breakdown of acts and scenes, the cast list, and the open stage directions, but not the play itself. Then they had to select one character from the cast list and write a paragraph predicting what would happen to that character in the play. Students selected characters, including Lena Younger, Ruth Younger, and Travis Younger. Then, drawing on their prior knowledge about the author and their understanding of the historical context in Chicago, as well as having viewed the documentary film *Hoop Dreams*, they wrote about what they thought that character would experience in the play. Reflecting later on this assignment, Tasha observed that students approached the text much more actively than usual. They read the stage directions very carefully and scanned the back for more details about the author. Looking ahead, Tasha commented that next time she would try to hook them more dramatically at the beginning by showing a short clip from the film version of the play and ask them to make a prediction. Then, she would give them the assignment to write a prediction about one character. Still, even in its present form, Tasha's approach helped her students understand the predictive dimension of reading at the same time that it prepared them for unexpected events in the play and for assessments that ask them to complete a narrative.

PLC ACTIVITY

Read the account of Tasha's lesson together as a group and consider the following:

- the goals she established
- the prior learning her students could draw upon
- the moves she made to prepare her students
- the activity students participated in
- Tasha's reflections on what she would do differently.

Then discuss how members of the group might adapt this lesson to their individual classes and compare the various directions that each takes.

The Pleasure of the Ambiguous

Many texts are not entirely clear, and part of the pleasure of reading is trying to figure them out. When Anne's book group read Julian Barnes' *The Sense of an Ending*, a novel in which an older man learns things that change his view of his younger self and of the people he knew at that period in his life, most of the discussion focused on unpacking the ambiguities. Questions about the reliability of the narrator, the sequence of revelations, and key phrases filled the room; everyone agreed it had been one of the best discussions ever. English is not the only subject with ambiguous texts. Primary documents in history often present different perspectives on the same event, and assignments can ask students to make an argument for one side or the other. Several released assessment items of PARCC and Smarter Balanced present students with texts that take different views and ask them to explore these in writing. One, for example, asks students to read several selections about nuclear waste and write an argument that draws on evidence from the texts. Developing the ability to write in response to questions like this, questions that may not have a clear right answer, can be fostered by helping students learn to read ambiguous texts. For older students, a story like "The Turn of the Screw" by Henry James can raise a number of questions that cannot be answered easily. For middle school students, a story like "The Telltale Heart" by Edgar Allen Poe can likewise help students learn to read ambiguous texts.

Reading for Information

Ask most high school students why they read, whether on Facebook or in a textbook, and they will probably say, "to find out about something." This rationale is echoed in the CCSS, with its emphasis on reading to gather information that can be used in writing. This is, of course, a reason why many people read. Reading offers a way of learning more about the world, of understanding others, of developing new capacities. Reading also supports more reading. When students read one text about the Civil War, they bring that background knowledge to their reading of another text on the same subject. It's a case of the rich getting richer. The more students read, the better they become at reading because they bring more background knowledge to every text they encounter.

RESEARCH AND POLITICAL CONSIDERATIONS

Research is central to the CCSS; several of the standards focus on it specifically, and it is also an essential part of writing more generally. Readers gather information and use it as evidence in their writing. An NCTE policy brief titled "Using Evidence in Writing" underscores the importance of helping students to incorporate evidence into their writing effectively, especially in an age of changing attitudes toward plagiarism. Among the research-based strategies that teachers can emphasize are:

- Relevancy: assessing whether the evidence is appropriately topical and timely
- Sufficiency: accounting for all evidence, including counterarguments, alternative perspectives, and/or conflicting reports
- Sourcing: noting the author (including his or her intentions) and context of the evidence
- Credibility: considering whether the source of the evidence offers expertise on the subject
- Accuracy and verifiability: judging whether the evidence is valid and trustworthy.

Online 5.1
Using Evidence in Writing

Sufficiency, accuracy, and verifiability are important strategies when writing on demand during the CCSS assessments. Students will be given some source texts to read; then they will have to decide how to use them when writing the essay. Some sources will be more accurate and useful than others. Students will have to discern the differences in credibility of sources and make decisions about what evidence to use, how much of it to use, and how to use it. Therefore, it is important that students have multiple opportunities to work with source texts prior to the assessment. A full copy of the NCTE brief is available in our online materials.

Even though a central reason for reading is to increase one's knowledge, it is important to help students develop a more nuanced understanding of reading. Many students assume that all reading is the same, that texts such as a web page, a textbook, a poem, or the back of a cereal box are identical. Similarly, many students assume that reading a novel for English class, a piece of primary research for history class, and a chemistry textbook are the same. To be sure, all of these require a basic ability to decode texts, but the strategies for approaching each text are different and the context (such as subject matter) introduces other variables. Because the CCSS emphasize text complexity, it will be especially important for teachers to help students develop more complex ways of thinking about reading. A first step is to help students identify additional reasons for reading.

Reading for Models

One of the most common reasons for reading that teachers offer is that it provides models for writing. If students have an opportunity to read excellent prose, the argument goes, they will begin to emulate it when they write. Although this approach to teaching writing has a long history, it has not always been successful because simply reading model texts does not necessarily translate into improved writing. The transfer from reading model texts to creating good writing is not automatic. Students need to learn strategies so that they can incorporate features from models into their own writing; they need to learn to read like writers.

Reading like a writer means paying close attention to *how* an author writes, to what strategies and techniques are being used, and to considering what one can learn about writing from reading. It makes reading more active, more participatory. As Mike Bunn puts it, "When you are reading like a writer, you are trying to figure out how the text you are reading was constructed so that you learn how to 'build' one for yourself" (Bunn 2011). Preparation is a good idea for any reading, but it is crucial for reading like a writer.

Before Reading

One of the first mistakes many student readers make is to simply pick up a text and start reading on the first page. Better readers know that it is important to develop an understanding of the context of the reading, to consider how the text is put together, and to see whether there are any special features. For example, a scientific article will have an abstract, figures, and charts, with the most important information near the end in the discussion or conclusion section, while a newspaper article will have a headline, dateline, and lead paragraph covering the essential points, with information presented in descending order of importance. Authors of scientific articles and newspaper articles expect readers to proceed differently, and learning to read well means understanding and using the structures provided by authors.

Part of becoming a more effective reader is developing an understanding of the multiplicity of text types. Different kinds of texts, sometimes called genres, can accomplish varying purposes. A poem, for example, is not often used to influence a legislator, but a scientific article could be. A legal brief can be very persuasive in a courtroom, but it would not be very effective in a religious service. Textbooks are used successfully to convey information in many classrooms, but they would not work well in a theatrical production. Students need to be exposed to different types of texts so they can learn to read a broader range of material. And, of course, reading a wide variety of types of writing will enable students to write in different genres.

One way to guide students toward reading more like writers is to have them write brief responses to the following questions as they examine texts before they start reading.

1. What are the parts of this text? How are they marked or identified?

2. What does the structure of the text tell you about its audience?

3. What does the author want to accomplish? How do you know?

4. What do you expect from this text?

5. What do you know about the context (time period, place, circumstances) in which this text was written?

6. Have you ever written a text like this? Could you?

Online 5.2
*Guiding
Questions for
Reading Like a
Writer*

During Reading

One of the challenges of reading is its invisibility. Some students who are daydreaming don't look any different from those who are actively engaged in reading a text. Although it is good to ask questions about a text before reading, it is equally good to keep asking questions during the process of reading, especially if the text is a model for student writers.

Asking and answering questions can help students stay focused and make their reading process more visible. This asking and answering of questions can also help students learn more about writing by paying attention to the strategies used by authors. They can learn to unpack the craft of other writers and begin to think about how they might replicate some of these effects in their own writing.

Here are some questions students can ask and answer as they are reading:

1. Does your view of what the author wants to accomplish change as you read? If so, how?

2. Does the text indicate the audience for which it is intended? If so, how?

3. How would you describe the degree of formality in the language of this text?

4. How does the author support claims made in this text?

5. What strategies does this author use to connect the parts of this text?

6. What works especially well in this text?

7. What questions remain when you finish reading?

Another strategy to help students read like writers is to assign two-column responses: In the left column they write sentences or phrases that strike them as especially good; then they explain why in the right column. Figure 5.1 shows an example from a student's reading of *Roll of Thunder, Hear My Cry* by Mildred D. Taylor.

Figure 5.1 Student Two-Column Response from *Roll of Thunder, Hear My Cry*

"Thank you for telling me Mr. Morrison. You're lucky no worse happened and we're glad to have you here … especially now" (p. 37).	Author shows Mama is frightened with just two words: "especially now."
Big Ma looked at me again, her voice cracking as she spoke. "Go on, child … apologize" (p. 115).	Author shows, with "voice cracking," that Cassie's grandmother doesn't want to make her apologize but has to.
Now you could be right 'bout Jeremy making a much finer friend than T.J. will ever be. The trouble is, down here in Mississippi, it costs too much to find out … (p. 158).	Author shows difficulty of black-white relationships in one sentence.

While all of these exercises help students build reading competence over the course of the year, when it comes to the CCSS assessment they will have to read strategically in a short amount of time. In piloting the CCSS, Ms. Helm found it useful for students to write the main focus of the prompt—"summarize the challenges Earhart faced"—at the top of the reading passage as they were reading. She made sure students had highlighters and instructed them to highlight the challenges as they read. Students could then draw from the highlighted passages when they were composing their essays. Novices often highlight too much as they are reading, so some instruction and modeling in strategic highlighting is helpful to students.

Notes on College Readiness

One of the capacities emphasized by the "Framework for Success in Post-secondary Writing" is critical thinking. To be ready for college, students need to develop their ability to think critically. The Framework explains that "*critical thinking* is the ability to analyze a situation or text and make thoughtful decisions based on that analysis." It further states:

> Writers use critical writing and reading to develop and represent the processes and products of their critical thinking. For example, writers may be asked to write about familiar or unfamiliar texts, examining assumptions about the texts held by different audiences. Through critical writing and reading, writers think through ideas, problems, and issues; identify and challenge assumptions; and explore multiple ways of understanding. This is important in college as writers are asked to move past obvious or surface-level interpretations and use writing to make sense of and respond to written, visual, verbal, and other texts that they encounter.

Like the CCSS, the Framework links reading and writing, making it clear that writers develop critical capacities as a result of careful attention to challenging texts.

Online 1.9
Framework for Success in Postsecondary Writing: Full Document

Strategies for Reading

In addition to the approaches to reading like a writer both before and during reading, there are other ways to help students read more proficiently. Every secondary school subject uses texts that have slightly different features, and making these visible to students is one way of helping them read more easily.

Understanding Subject Area Differences

As students move from class to class throughout the day, they encounter many different kinds of reading challenges. Each subject requires different approaches to texts. English classes require students to read and understand poems; to analyze novels; to read plays with lists of characters, dialogue, and stage directions; and to gather information from a variety of nonfiction texts. The arrangement of words in a poem, for instance, can seem so obvious that it's not worth mentioning, but arrangement conveys information about reading. The relatively small number of words in a poem indicates the importance of considering each one carefully, just as the use of lines and breaks signals that the sound and rhythm of language matter.

Classroom Moves

Ask students to read a poem like Frost's "Nothing Gold Can Stay," and write a prose explanation of each line. They can compare their "readings" with peers and then discuss with the class how each line contributes to the meaning of the whole poem.

> *Nature's first green is gold,*
> *Her hardest hue to hold.*
> *Her early leaf's a flower;*
> *But only so an hour.*
> *Then leaf subsides to leaf.*
> *So Eden sank to grief,*
> *So dawn goes down to day.*
> *Nothing gold can stay.*
>
> —*Robert Frost*

Social Studies

Students in social studies courses need to read a variety of primary documents as well as textbooks, tables, and charts. Primary documents often contain unfamiliar and/or archaic language that can make reading difficult. Many students will need help in learning how to approach the texts required in social studies classes. Give students copies of the excerpt from *Narrative of the Life of Frederick Douglass, An American Slave, Written by Himself* which is available on our online site.

Online 5.3
Narrative of the Life of Frederick Douglass

Ask them to imagine that they need to help a younger student prepare to read it. Tell them to list the background information readers will need, the words that will need explanation, and the concepts they will need to understand. Then ask them to share and discuss their lists.

Science

Visual texts such as tables, charts, graphs, and diagrams take on special importance in science courses. Specialists in science often claim that they look first at the visual portion of texts to understand their gist and then turn to the prose simply for confirmation and elaboration. Teachers in science courses need to help students understand how to read such visual texts effectively.

Use the image, Tsunami diagram, in Figure 5.2 or another page from a science text that contains visual information. Ask students to look only at the visual information and write an explanation of what it tells them. Then have them compare and discuss their explanations.

Figure 5.2 Tsunami Diagram

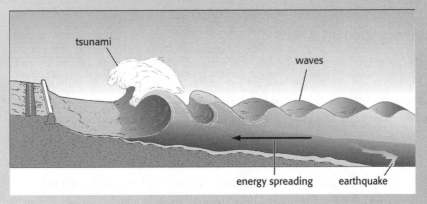

© Houghton Mifflin Harcourt

This image is also available in this book's online resources.

Online 5.4
Tsunami Diagram

Reading Digital Texts

The increased use of digital technologies in classrooms has many advantages for teaching and learning, but it also requires specific help with reading. For example, the arrangement of words on websites has led to what brain researchers call an F pattern, where the eye first scans the left side from top to bottom and then sweeps across from left to right at a couple of different levels. It will help students to know that this can be a very efficient way of gathering information from a website.

Reading Textbooks

Textbooks in all subjects provide a number of cues for reading. The use of headings and subheadings organizes information within chapters. Boxed quotations pulled from the text, images, graphic organizers, and charts all serve to guide reading. Questions and review notes at the end of chapters can help students monitor their own reading. However, many students will not know how to take advantage of these cues unless they have specific guidance for doing so.

Part of reading instruction at the secondary level, then, involves helping students identify and use the graphic and visual features of various kinds of texts in order to make meaning. Since each high school subject employs different sorts of texts, teachers in each subject are best able to help students learn to read most effectively in that area. Strategies for using graphic and visual features to read a lab report, an editorial or policy brief, or a script for a play are best explained by science, social studies, and English teachers respectively.

Discerning Structural Markers

Texts can be organized in many different ways, and patterns of organization are indicated by language. The overall message of an informational text is often summarized near the beginning, to give readers a frame through which they can read what follows. Helping students to see how this kind of framing works can enable them to read more efficiently. Here, for example, is the first paragraph of an article about how one person became a scientist:

> Before I was born, my father told my mother, "If it's boy, he's going to be a scientist." When I was just a little kid, very small in a highchair, my father brought home a lot of little bathroom tiles—seconds—of different colors.

We played with them, my father setting them up vertically on my highchair like dominoes, and I would push one end so they would all go down.

—*Richard Feynman*

Ask students to read a passage like this and write an explanation of what they expect the following paragraphs to be about as well as what clues they draw on to reach this decision.

Structural markers within the body of informational texts often include signal words such as *first, second,* and *third* to indicate key pieces of information that contribute to a larger definition or claim. Alternatively, some texts include signal words such as *in contrast, alternatively,* or *instead* that indicate similarities and differences between concepts or positions being advanced. Another set of signal words such as *because, as a result,* or *since* can indicate causal relationships, alerting readers to ways that ideas are connected. Similarly, words like *if/then* or *when/thus* can signal problems and solutions or issues and resolutions.

Most informational texts use signal words in combination with other structures to provide connections or coherence for readers. *Repetition* of key terms or phrases is one way that readers can determine what is most important in a text. *Placement*, usually at the beginning or end of paragraphs or sections, is another structural marker that can inform reading. Parenthetical or appositional *definitions*, as in a definition surrounded by commas, also serve to guide readers.

Some texts, of course, do not include signal words, or they have some signal words combined with logical structures that can guide students. Students can read passages and identify the progressions in the text, pointing to the logical moves the author makes to give structure to the writing. Kevin Galvin, a science teacher, did this with his students. With CCSS ELA-Literacy. RST. 9-10.1 ("Cite specific textual evidence to support analysis of science and technical texts, attending to the precise details of explanations or descriptions" and CCSS ELA-Literacy. RT.9-10.2 "Determine the central ideas or conclusions of a text; trace the text's explanation or depiction of a complex process, phenomenon, or concept; provide an accurate summary of the text") in mind, he asked students to read an article about dinosaurs and use signal words as well as logical moves to follow the argument. Then, following the model of a PARCC sample assessment that requires students to read an article and identify central claims, he asked them to write paragraphs in which they identified a central claim and provided reasoning that linked their evidence to that claim.

In reflecting on this assignment, Kevin felt that it achieved his goal of having students analyze a text and look for evidence to support a claim about the text. Looking ahead, Kevin said that his next assignment would ask students to read a more complex article to move their claim, evidence, and reasoning to a higher level. Kevin also noted that the PARCC assessment prototype and rubric were limited in that they did not assess students' reasoning skills, something he wants his students to develop.

Identifying Rhetorical Strategies

In addition to structural markers that signal how a text is organized, students can learn to identify rhetorical strategies that help to create specific effects in writing. It is valuable to students to develop a vocabulary so they can identify rhetorical strategies that contribute to texts and use these features to improve their own writing. Some of the most common strategies are shown in Figure 5.3.

Online 5.5
*Common
Rhetorical
Strategies*

Figure 5.3 Common Rhetorical Strategies

Allusion	Enriches by referring to another text. "It rained for 40 days" refers to the story of Noah.
Antithesis	Adds drama by placing opposing concepts together. "It was the best of times, it was the worst of times."
Foreshadowing	Presents information to prepare the reader for later claims or actions. A sentence like "Dinosaurs were in decline before an asteroid hit 65.5 million years ago" foreshadows what follows in the article.
Hyperbole	Uses exaggeration to create an effect. "I can smell pizza from a mile away."
Incremental repetition	Employs repetition for effect. "And it was easy to conclude that a bad man will do bad things, even if there is insufficient evidence for one bad thing in particular."
Metaphor	Contains an implied comparison. "She is drowning in a sea of grief."
Parallelism	Adds symmetry and balance to writing. "The car was not just what I wanted but also just what I needed."
Personification	Assigns human qualities to something non-human. "When opportunity knocks, be sure to open the door."

Accounting for Language Variation and Vocabulary

One of the challenges of text-based writing in secondary school is that the language becomes more specialized. Each subject has its own way of expressing ideas, and students need to negotiate unfamiliar terms at the same time that they are learning new concepts. Consider, for example, the following passages.

> In the olde dayes of the Kyng Arthour,
> Of which that Britons speken grert honour,
> Al was this land fulfild of fayeryë.

> Today we will use Riemann sums and definite integrals to find the volume of a solid by using slicing.

> No Senator or Representative shall, during the Time for which he was elected, be appointed to any civil Office under the Authority of the United States, which shall have been created, or the Emoluments whereof shall have been encreased during such time; and no Person holding any Office under the United States, shall be a Member of either House during his Continuance in Office.

> The Krebs acid cycle is a series of enzymatic reactions in mitochondria involving oxidative metabolism of acetyl compounds to produce high-energy phosphate compounds that are the source of cellular energy.

Any of the language reproduced above could be required reading for a high school student, and this array is only a small sample of the varieties of English that students may need to read. Not only do students need to learn new vocabulary, but within a given disciplinary context familiar words can take on new meaning. For example, in the excerpt from the calculus assignment, *slicing* does not mean cutting with a knife. Terms like *emoluments* and *civil office* or *mitochondria* and *acetyl compounds* do not occur commonly in everyday speech, but they can be essential for reading within a given field. Because language is always changing, the spellings and meanings of words also shift across time, and student readers need to be apprised of these variations also. The word *fulfild*, now spelled *fulfilled*, meant "present everywhere" in the fifteenth century when Chaucer was writing, even though we currently use it to mean accomplished.

Acknowledging the multiplicity of language and concepts that are necessary, and helping students develop strategies for addressing them, will lead to more effective text-based writing.

Figure 5.4 Joos' Five Levels of Formality

Level	Characteristics of Language
Frozen	The words are always the same. Examples: the Lord's Prayer, the Pledge of Allegiance.
Formal	The word choice and sentence structure used by the business and education community. Uses a 1,200-word to 1,600-word spoken vocabulary. Example: "This assignment is not acceptable in its present format."
Consultative	A mix of formal and casual register. Example: "I can't accept the assignment the way it is."
Casual	Language used between friends, which comes out of the oral tradition. Contains few abstract words and uses nonverbal assists. Example: "This work is a no-go. Can't take it."
Intimate	Private language shared between two individuals, such as family members, boyfriends, or girlfriends.

In addition to an array of new terms and concepts, secondary school students also encounter differences in register or the degree of formality in language. Helping them recognize a range of registers will prepare them to read a wide variety of texts. The five levels of formality identified by Martin Joos suggest the range of registers that may appear in texts students read.

Calling Upon Prior Knowledge

It is easy to assume that being a reader means having the skills for extracting meaning from a text, but the degree to which students are able to make meaning with texts also depends on the knowledge they bring to the texts. Readers who have a background in biology will find it much easier to comprehend the definition of the Krebs acid cycle than those who know nothing about this area of science. Likewise, readers who know something about U.S. government will find it easier to read the excerpt from the U.S. Constitution than readers more familiar with another form of government.

Prior knowledge can derive from previous learning in subjects like science or social studies, but it can also be drawn from students' experiences outside of school. The student who comes from a Muslim family will probably be knowledgeable about rituals of fasting and charitable giving while a student from a Christian family will be more likely to understand references to Noah's ark or a prodigal son. Helping students to understand their own cultural knowledge as a resource for reading is another way of preparing students for text-based writing.

Attending to Openings

> When in the course of human events, it becomes necessary for one people to dissolve the political bands which have connected them with another …

> Four score and seven years ago our fathers brought forth on this continent a new nation conceived in liberty and dedicated to the proposition that all men are created equal.

> It is a truth universally acknowledged, that a single man in possession of a good fortune, must be in want of a wife.

> Call me Ishmael.

> It was the best of times, it was the worst of times …

> I am an invisible man.

> There was once a town in the heart of America where all life seemed to live in harmony with its surroundings.

> On January 29, 1951, David Lacks sat behind the wheel of his old Buick, watching the rain fall.

Chances are you easily recognize a number of the texts from which these opening lines were taken. Representatives of the thirteen American colonies, Jane Austen, Abraham Lincoln, Herman Melville, Charles Dickens, Ralph Ellison, Rachel Carson, and Rebecca Skloot each demonstrate what good writers know. Openings matter. Hook a reader with an engaging opening and that reader is yours. But openings do more than get readers' attention; they introduce readers to what will follow, they offer hints and promises, they enable readers to make predictions.

The first sentence of the Declaration of Independence ended with this: "and to assume among the powers of the earth, the separate and equal station to which the Laws of Nature and of Nature's God entitle them, a decent respect to the opinions of mankind requires that they should declare the causes which impel them to the separation." With this opening sentence the representatives of the thirteen colonies made clear the purpose of the document they were all signing.

In novels, openings often suggest themes that will be played out in what follows as, for example, the narrative surrounding the wealthy Darby in *Pride and Prejudice*. Indeed each of these opening lines evokes much of what follows in the novel. Openings in other forms of writing also help to establish much of what follows. Joan Didion, for example, opens her essay "Good-bye to All That," with this line: "It is easy to see the beginnings of things, and harder to see the ends" (1980, 317). With this one deceptively simple sentence, Didion intrigues the reader, suggests the general subject, communicates an attitude, and forecasts where the essay will go.

By beginning the Gettysburg Address with a reminder of the larger goals of the United States as a nation, Abraham Lincoln created a rhetorical context that extended beyond the many dead soldiers he was present to memorialize. This stance differs significantly from the one Rebecca Skloot takes in introducing *The Immortal Life of Henrietta Lacks*, beginning with a small domestic moment to launch an account of a very significant event in medical science.

In addition to considering how openings shape the reading that follows, it is also useful to consider the craft of openings. What is the effect of the imperative of the first line of *Moby-Dick*? How would that effect change if the line were "You can call me Ishmael" or "My name is Ishmael"? How does the effect of this imperative compare with the declarative "I am an invisible man"?

The full sentence that opens *A Tale of Two Cities* is: "It was the best of times, it was the worst of times, it was the age of wisdom, it was the age of foolishness, it was the epoch of belief, it was the epoch of incredulity, it was the season of Light, it was the season of Darkness, it was the spring of hope, it was the winter of despair." Consider the syntax of this sentence, how Dickens uses an extended sequence of paired contrasts to make his point. How would the opening change if the last four pairs were eliminated? If it read, "It was the best and worst of times, the age of wisdom and foolishness" and so on? And how does this narrative opening resemble and differ from that used by Rachel Carson in *Silent Spring*?

Students can explore various other possibilities for modifying this opening and considering the different effects. Some students may not see immediate differences, but with practice they can begin to notice that something changes with each variation. The goal here is to encourage students to pay closer attention to what they are reading and, at the same time, to make them aware that they know more about sentence structure and word choice than they may have realized.

Online 5.6
*Fill-in-the-Blanks
Sentence Exercise*

Another exercise to foster more awareness of how openings work is to use the basic structure of an opening to play with versions of a fill-in-the blank model. Doing this can help students learn to read more closely and to develop more flexibility in their writing.

Students can experiment with the blanks and compare the sentences they create using the model. This succession of models offers less and less support for students.

Model 1

It was the best of _____, it was the worst of _____, it was the age of _____, it was the age of_____, it was the epoch of_____, it was the season of_____, it was the season of _____, it was the spring of _____, it was the winter of _____.

Model 2

It was the _____, it was the_____, it was the_____, it was the _____, it was the _____, it was the _____, it was the _____, it was the _____, it was the _____.

Model 3

It was_____ _____, it was_____ _____, it was_____ _____, it was _____ _____, it was _____ _____, it was _____ _____, it was _____ _____, it was _____ _____, it was _____ _____, it was _____ _____.

Examining Closings

Students know that effective closings summarize what has gone before and give readers a satisfying end. In that sense, closings are easier to write than openings. Key points have been made, and all that is needed is a restatement. But truly effective closings do something extra; they offer readers more than a restatement or summary.

For teachers, helping students understand closings or conclusions is more difficult than dealing with openings. Out of context, closings often do not make sense or reveal their craft. Students must read or consider the entire piece that precedes it to really see the value of the closing because without that context the effect of conclusions can be lost.

The conclusion to James Baldwin's "Stranger in the Village," for example, will be impressive only if a reader knows that the essay focuses on an African American man's brief residence in a Swiss village where no black man had ever been seen. Baldwin moves from one village to the world and declares that the universe is unalterably changed with this closing:

"The world is white no longer, and it will never be white again" (1933 77).

Yet, even with a bit of context, the full effect of Baldwin's closing is not as clear as it is to those who have read the entire essay.

Another example of a closing is offered by Gertrude Reiss's essay "Naftale," in which the author asks her father to tell her about his life. The incidents are recounted without interpretation and comment, and it is only through the one-sentence conclusion that the reader understands the whole essay:

> "Until I asked my father to tell me about his life, I never knew he was a happy man" (1997, 52).

This closing illuminates the entire essay, revealing the point of everything that has gone before. But the difficulty of seeing this without reading the entire essay suggests that teachers do best to have students read whole pieces so they can get the sense of the power of a conclusion.

Classroom Moves

Teachers can do a number of things to help students become more aware of the variety of things closings can do. Here is a list of options:

1. Restate or summarize major points.
2. Offer a final, clincher point.
3. Emphasize one particular insight.
4. Cite the broad significance or deeper implications of the main points.
5. Make a prediction.
6. Recommend how information can be applied.
7. Tell a pertinent story, ask a question, or cite an authority.

When students have a firm understanding of why they are reading as well as a repertoire of strategies to use, they can become effective readers in a variety of contexts. In reading as in economics, the rich become richer. Students who read more become better readers, and teachers in every subject can contribute to that development. In this chapter we have shown how students can be taught to read for the information they need to write with source texts, but we have also shown how students can be taught to read for the craft of language. It is this knowledge of craft that they can apply in their own writing, not only to strengthen their openings and closings but to make their prose more powerful overall.

Chapter Six

Using Assessment to Improve Writing Instruction

CHAPTER OVERVIEW *This chapter provides strategies for:*

- *distinguishing formative from summative assessment*

- *writing in science*

- *conferring with student writers*

- *implementing peer review*

- *enacting self-evaluation.*

ecause high-stakes assessment has been so controversial, especially when it is tied to teacher evaluation, it is easy to forget how valuable assessment can be for improving teaching. Assessment provides an indication of what students have learned, where they encounter difficulties in understanding, and how they need to improve. Effective assessment informs instruction, giving teachers ideas about what to emphasize, how to allocate time, and which resources to call upon. This chapter considers several different kinds of assessment, suggesting how each can improve the teaching of writing.

Formative and Summative Assessment

As the definitions in Chapter 2 show, there are two main types of assessment: (1) formative assessment, which occurs during the process of writing and provides feedback that can be used to develop further writing, and (2) summative assessment, which occurs after writing has been completed and results in a grade or score. The advantages of summative assessment include its finality: It provides a clear endpoint with an indication of a student's performance. It also offers a means of comparing students' performances both within and across groups, as well as across time.

One of the challenges posed by summative evaluation is to avoid employing it too soon. Anyone who has seen students look at their grade at the end of a paper and then throw it away, or has seen stacks of graded papers that students don't bother to pick up, knows that once a grade is assigned, learning stops. Since writing is a process that takes time, writing instructors need to give students an opportunity to experience the learning that accompanies each stage in the process. This doesn't mean that no assessment occurs during the processes of writing, but it does mean that final grades or scores are not assigned until students have time to learn from the process.

A Formative Approach

Consider, for example, how Paula Gentile, a biology teacher, gave her students time to learn from the processes of writing by employing formative assessment before she moved to summative evaluation. Paula's students were juniors in a general biology class, students she describes as close to the middle in terms of their primary academic skills. Her goals were to help her students understand current schemata regarding climate change and human impact on global warming. She also wanted her students to learn to synthesize information from multiple sources in order to write a persuasive essay. Her thinking was influenced by both the CCSS Standards for Literacy in Science and Technical Subjects as well as the model of assessment in Partnership for Assessment of Readiness for College and Careers' (PARCC's) Research Simulation Task (see Chapter 7 for an example of this task). She recognized that students would need both factual and conceptual knowledge to do this writing; she also knew that they would need to use the following modes of analysis:

- differentiating relevant from irrelevant material
- integrating information from multiple sources
- identifying coherence in the information available in order to organize it
- determining multiple perspectives in the information available.

Paula's overall goals were to prepare students to (1) scaffold their understanding of how to organize and apply factual and conceptual knowledge in writing, and (2) provide a format through which they could learn to analyze knowledge, breaking it into components that would extend their comprehension and engage them in higher-order thinking. Her more specific goals were to support students in (1) identifying and expressing current schemata relative to climate change and human impact on global warming, and (2) constructing evidence-based claims in a formal written form, similar to what they would encounter in CCSS assessments. She knew that her students would need the support of formative assessment in writing because they had little experience with responding to the kinds of summative writing assessments represented by PARCC and Smarter Balanced Assessment Consortium (SBAC). She also knew that formative assessment does not mean simply giving students a pre-test or a model based on a summative assessment.

RESEARCH AND POLITICAL CONSIDERATIONS

The term *formative assessment* is used frequently in discussions of CCSS assessments, but it is not always distinguished carefully from repeated summative assessments. A policy research brief published by the National Council of Teachers of English uses the term *high-quality formative assessment* to distinguish it from formative assessment that is merely a preview of summative assessment. The features that characterize high-quality formative assessment include the following:

- It emphasizes the quality rather than the quantity of student work.

- It prizes giving advice and guidance over giving grades.

- It avoids comparing students in favor of enabling individual students to assess their own learning.

- It fosters dialogues that explore understandings rather than lectures that present information.

- It encourages multiple iterations of an assessment cycle, each focused on a few issues.

- It provides feedback that engenders motivation and leads to improvement.

A copy of this entire brief is available in our online materials and can be used in discussions about ways to develop and enhance approaches to formative assessment.

Online 6.1
*Fostering
High Quality
Formative
Assessment*

With a clear understanding of formative assessment, Paula began preparing her students for summative assessment in writing by engaging them in a sequence of formative assessments. To introduce the topic, she showed a video that discussed climate change and its impact. A link to that video is available in our online materials.

Online 6.2
*Video on Climate
Change*

She gave her students about a minute to think about whether the clip challenged any ideas they already had or raised any questions for them. After this pause, students filled in answers to the questions in column one of the graphic organizer shown in Figure 6.1. When they finished this individual writing, students paired up to answer the same questions in column two, but this time they had an opportunity to exchange ideas with one another. Before class ended, Paula led a discussion of the reflection questions along with the responses generated by her students in response to columns one and two.

Notice that to complete column two, students need to come to some agreement, which means that each member of the pair needs to understand the other's viewpoint. Paula collected the graphic organizers at the end of class and read them that evening, looking for gaps in comprehension, significant misconceptions, and the level of conceptual understanding demonstrated in student writing. She used the information she gathered to inform her instruction the next day and to shape the note-taking session that followed.

Online 6.3
*Climate Change:
Exploring Our
Understanding of
Global Warming*

Figure 6.1 Climate Change: Exploring Our Understanding of Global Warming

Questions	Preliminary Ideas Your independent perspective	Pair and Share Collaborate to combine views	Supporting Your Perspective Adding evidence to support definitions and claims
How would you describe/explain global warming? What is it?			
What do you believe contributes to (causes) global warming? Be specific! You cannot simply say "humans" or "nature."			
What do you think people and/or governments should do about global warming?			

On the next day, Paula engaged her students in interactive note-taking while she presented basic information about climate change. Students were given a modified version of Paula's PowerPoint presentation (with headings and images but no content). The full PowerPoint presentation is available in our online materials, but the sample that follows shows one of the slides in the form students received.

Online 6.4
Climate Change Mini-Lecture PowerPoint

NOTES	
	Climate vs. Weather
	What is weather?
	What is climate?

With a series of guiding questions, she helped students build the content for each slide and annotate each image so they could call upon their visual abilities to make connections between factual and procedural understanding. This form of note-taking enabled students to process the information they were being given so that it was more likely they would be able to remember and use it in their writing.

The next activity was to create a timeline. Paula chose this activity as a way of helping students understand how to use evidence to support their definitions and claims. She gave pairs of students one or two events or discoveries in the history of climate change and told them to paraphrase the information in their own words on a piece of construction paper. The full timeline is available in our online materials.

Online 6.5
Global Warming Timeline Fact Sheet

Items included information about famous scientists and their discoveries as well as significant natural events. Then, the whole class went through the events/discoveries in ascending order, with each student pair adding its piece of construction paper, thereby building understanding of climate change with each item added to the timeline. After the timeline was created, the class analyzed it, with two objectives: (1) to summarize its meaning and implication, and (2) to identify whether it was an example of data from scientific research/observation [D] or a political perspective [P] and whether it suggested human-based causes [H] or a natural phenomenon [N]. This process enabled students to incorporate evidence into column three of their graphic organizers.

On the following day, the class watched another documentary on climate change, with Paula pausing the film frequently to reiterate concepts discussed previously, clarify misconceptions, and probe student understanding. For example, many students assume that climate change and global warming are the same thing, not understanding that climate change is a factor in global warming; this leads them to question whether global warming is "real" since we still have cold winters.

With this combination of writing, class discussions and dialogues designed to foster understanding, opportunities for students to distinguish among various kinds of evidence, and multiple iterations of self- and teacher-assessment, Paula decided that her students were ready for summative assessment. Here is the assignment students were given:

> Using the information you have gathered from (1) our class notes, (2) the documentary clip, and (3) the timeline of events that we created as a class, construct an essay response to the following question:
>
> *Do you believe the United States government should be more aggressive in addressing the issue of global warming? Why or why not?*
>
> (You may use your perspectives/evidence chart to help you in constructing your response.)
>
> 1. Begin by stating your claim (I believe the U.S. government …)
>
> 2. Then, using complete sentences, explain at least three pieces of evidence from our timeline that support your claim. This should be written with a minimum of three sentences.
>
> 3. Conclude your paragraph with a summary statement that reiterates your position.

As you can see, Paula's students did several kinds of writing before they began the essay, and Paula assessed each, not to assign a grade but to determine where her students needed help with learning. This high-quality formative assessment guided students from one step to another in learning. The graphic organizer, interactive note-taking, timeline, and pausing approach to video clips didn't require students to write a lot, but it was writing that emphasized learning. In responding to students' writing, Paula made suggestions and offered corrections, but she didn't assign grades to any of this work, and she wasn't comparing students to one another. The rich mixture of writing and class discussions about climate change helped students develop factual and conceptual understandings and, at the same time, moved them toward greater facility with writing because they had opportunities to write in a variety of forms for multiple purposes.

A Summative Approach

In turning to summative assessment, Paula created a rubric designed to measure the learning goals she had established for her students (see Figure 6.2).

Although Paula's students did not help to create the rubric, they each had a copy to guide them when they were writing in response to the prompt she had created.

Figure 6.2 Grading Rubric

Component	Missing	Insufficient	Satisfactory
Claim	No claim stated.	An idea is presented but not phrased as a claim and/or does not use the sentence starter.	Claim is clearly stated using the designated sentence starter.
Evidence	No evidence from the timeline is incorporated or explained.	1–2 pieces of evidence from the timeline are explained or 3 pieces of evidence are explained but do not all support the claim.	3 pieces of evidence from the timeline are explained in support of the claim.
Conclusion	No concluding statement is included.	Concluding statement is incorporated but does not reiterate the position/claim.	Concluding statement incorporated that reiterates the position/claim.
Format/grammar	Incomplete sentences (fragments); numerous misspellings and poor grammar.	Mostly complete sentences; some spelling/grammar mistakes.	Written with complete sentences and contains few, if any, spelling/grammar mistakes.

Here are three examples of writing produced by Paula's students, along with a summary of the comments she made on each.

Student A's Writing

I believe the U.S. government should be more aggressive in addressing the issue of global warming because if they don't our world will be over-polluted and destroyed. Back in the 1890s, a Swedish scientist suggested that the burning of fossil fuels could lead to global warming. His suggestion led to what the world is now. If the government doesn't crack down on the issue of global warming the man-made changes could bring major climate changes. For example, rising temperatures and sea levels will cause major flooding and catastrophic storms. The government should be more aggressive.

In responding to Student A, Paula praised the connection to early predictions with contemporary discussions of climate change and the use of examples to support claims made.

Student B's Writing

I believe that the U.S. government should push the issue of global warming. I believe this because in 1957 Davis Neeling discovered that the level of carbon dioxide in the atmosphere was going up. Then in 1985 NASA climate scientist James Hanson and team reported that the earth's temperature was going up more and the biggest contributor was the gases that we humans caused. Then in 2008, the third hottest year on record, the heat caused the death of 30,000 people.

Paula's response to Student B called for an explanation of how humans contribute to rising temperatures on earth, asked for better transitions between sentences, and noted the lack of a conclusion but praised the use of evidence.

Student C's Writing

I believe the US government should be more aggressive in addressing the issue of global warming. Gilbert Plass, a Canadian physicist wrote a book that stated that humans are the reason that global warming is becoming a bigger issue. Also, industrial plants and the burning of fossil fuels are one of the many reasons for global warming. In conclusion humans do increase the amount of carbon dioxide that gets trapped in the atmosphere.

In responding to Student C Paula asked for an explanation of what contributed to the greenhouse effect and called for reasons to explain why humans are described as accelerating global warming and asked how the concluding statement connects to the original statement.

In keeping with principles of summative assessment, each of these papers received a grade as well as Paula's comments, enabling Paula to compare the performances of individual students with one another and, at the same time, give students a ranked indication of the quality of their work. In Paula's view, student A's mini-essay was most successful, B a little less so, and C among the least successful. However, even student C's essay met the basic requirements, and Paula was pleased by the way students were able to incorporate evidence from their study of climate change to support their positions regarding the government's approach to climate change. The ability to construct claims supported by research-based evidence is critical in science and is a fundamental skill for CCSS assessments. Since this was her students' first experience with writing evidence-based essays, Paula felt that they had been very successful. In reflecting on how she would improve future implementations of this assignment, Paula indicated that she would provide students with a sample of a similar essay written in response to another prompt so that students could see an example of her expectations for incorporating the information, and she would add a day of peer feedback and revision in order to scaffold students' ability to improve their writing.

Classroom Moves

Select two or three of the types of formative assessment Paula used—graphic organizer, interactive note-taking, timeline, or pausing approach to video clips—and adapt them to the subject you are teaching. After you have used this sequence of formative assessments in class, write a reflection on what students' responses showed you about their learning, and how that, in turn, shaped your teaching.

Conferencing

Talking with students individually about their writing is one of the most powerful forms of formative assessment. Research shows that this is a highly effective way to help students learn from processes of writing and to enable them to become more effective writers. Among other things, it prepares students to become better judges of their own writing, which is essential for them to succeed as writers in multiple contexts, including assessments like those of PARCC and Smarter Balanced. It can, of course, seem impossible to talk with individual students about their drafts in classes of thirty students, but teachers can do it if conferences are kept brief and are conducted while other reading and writing activities are going on. Let's imagine that students are working on their writing, and the teacher is available, at a desk, for 5-minute conferences with students who have been identified for the day's conferences. The teacher could, conceivably, confer with seven or eight students and still have time, during a regular class period, to circulate through the classroom or do a minilesson for the entire class.

The best conferences are those that are directed by students, so that they can learn to identify features that need attention in their own writing. Here are some questions that teachers can ask to help students lead conferences:

- What do you want to work on today?
- What parts of the assignment do you find challenging?
- What do you think about what you have already written?
- What do you want to do next with this piece of writing?
- How can I help you today?

These questions and others like them share an emphasis on helping students to look closely at their own writing. When conferences are student directed, teachers do not focus on correcting or improving drafts; rather, they encourage students to identify what they see as important to work on. To be sure, some students will need prompting to become proficient leaders in conferences. Teachers can help by asking even more specific questions such as these:

- Would you like to look at the first sentence?
- Can you show me the part that you like best?
- Can you show me a sentence or part you have a question about?
- What question do you have for me?

Sometimes students will ask for help with specific issues such as punctuation or sentence structure; then, it is appropriate for the teacher to provide direct instruction. Otherwise, however, the teacher needs to resist the impulse to help students "fix" their writing. A student-led conference, even when guided by teacher questions, will enable students to learn much more than a list of corrections a teacher might offer. Student-led conferences help develop more independent and self-aware writers. This, in turn, prepares students to write more effectively in high-stakes assessments like those of PARCC and SBAC as well as many other contexts of writing.

Peer Review

In some ways, peer review can be seen as a type of formative assessment because it leads students toward knowing how to assess their own writing. It provides feedback and an immediate audience response that can motivate students to improve their drafts, and it fosters conversations about writing that deepens understandings. However, peer review can also be considered as a distinct type of assessment because it takes multiple forms, it is uniquely able to enhance students' understanding of audience, and it enables students to experience the social or collaborative dimensions of writing. Too often, students see writing as something done in isolation from others, as very rigid in form and content, and as directed to the teacher alone.

Peer review can inspire fear in both teacher and students. Teachers worry that students will get out of control when they meet in groups by wasting time because they don't know what to do or do nothing except share their ignorance about writing. Students often share these fears. They are accustomed to following directions from the teacher and worry about knowing what to do. Able writers often resent working with students who don't write as well as well as they do, claiming that they won't get any real help with their writing. "It's the teacher's job to help me with my writing," they will say. Teachers, in turn, may fear that they are not doing their jobs if they aren't responding directly to everything their students write.

These fears can all be addressed. When the purposes and tasks of peer-response writing groups are made clear to students, there is little real chance that students will either get out of control or get lost. Part of the teacher's responsibility is to scaffold students' experiences with peer review so they are ready for the challenges of group work. One important early step is to model peer review for students, for example, by doing a whole-class workshop with a piece of student writing from another class so that students can begin learning the language of response. A guide like the one shown in Figure 6.3 can give students a clear idea of what they are expected to do, and students can also use it to evaluate others in their own groups.

The best response to the concern about more able students not benefitting from the comments of their peers is to make it clear that the greatest benefit of peer response is not the responses to one's own writing but the opportunity to look closely at the writing of others. Just as it is easier to see personality flaws in others rather than ourselves, it is

Online 6.6
Peer-Review
Rubric

Figure 6.3 Peer-Review Rubric

Reviewer's name: _____

Author's name (include all if more than one): _____

Document title: _____

Hour: _____ Date: _____

Criteria	Not evidenced	Insufficient	Sufficient	Expected
Submitted *your* finished paper to your reviewers by the review day deadline.	0 points	2 points— Incomplete/not finished/or past deadline.	7 points— Fully complete paper in by the deadline, but supporting documents missing.	10 points— Fully complete paper in by the deadline with all supporting documents.
Provided meaningful feedback on data/research sufficiency.	0 points	2 points— Comments are superficial and do not provide true analysis.	4 points— Comments indicate correct analysis of the data/research.	5 points— Comments include specific suggestions, references to evidence for suggestions, and additional resources for consideration (from course materials).

Figure 6.3 Peer-Review Rubric *(continued)*

Criteria	Not evidenced	Insufficient	Sufficient	Expected
Provided meaningful feedback on structure, organization, and clarity of points.	0 points	2 points— Comments are superficial and do not provide constructive feedback that can be used by authors.	4 points— Comments clearly identify potential problems with the structures and organization of the components.	5 points— Comments include specific suggestions for improving structure, order, and content.
Provided meaningful feedback on the logic, assumptions, and recommendations of the author(s).	0 points	2 points— Comments provided are not logical or incorrectly state assumptions.	4 points— Comments illustrate useful analysis of logic/ assumptions and identify potential problems.	5 points— Comments include specific suggestions for improving/ resolving problems with logic/ assumptions and help to restate recommendations that are better supported by the evidence.
Provided all comments in a positive, encouraging, and constructive manner.	0 points	2 points— Comments are neutral or not encouraging.	4 points— Comments include positive feedback and suggestions.	5 points— Comments praise specific strengths of the paper (and supporting documents) as well as constructively address weaknesses, with alternatives that might be considered.

easier to see problems in the writing of others; the process of learning to evaluate others' writing strengthens the capacity to see one's own writing more clearly.

Since English language arts teachers are more likely to have experience with peer reviews, teachers in other disciplines may feel hesitant about using this strategy. However, peer-review writing groups can be used effectively in any subject. Figure 6.4, as an example, shows guidelines Paula created for students in science classes.

Online 6.7
Peer-Review Rubric for Writing in the Sciences

Figure 6.4 Peer-Review Rubric for Writing in the Sciences

Reviewer's name: _____

Author's name (include all if more than one): _____

Document title: _____

Hour: _____   Date: _____

Introduction Section	Yes/No/Partially	Explanation	Comments/Feedback/Suggestions
Is the main idea/focal topic clearly introduced and is significance explicitly stated/ explained?			
Does the author summarize relevant previous research?			
Is there sufficient evidence to support all claims?			
Are in-text citations used correctly to document sources of information and evidence?			

Figure 6.4 Peer-Review Rubric for Writing in the Sciences *(continued)*

Introduction Section	Yes/No/Partially	Explanation	Comments/Feedback/ Suggestions
Is the objective of the current study clearly stated at the end of the section, with indications for the purpose and overall goal(s)?			

Methods Section	Yes/No/Partially	Explanation	Comments/Feedback/ Suggestions
Are the methods clearly outlined in paragraph form such that you could replicate the study? Are supporting illustrations, tables, and/ or graphs included, with proper captions and in-text references? Are units, quantities, and values included where necessary to fully explain the steps and materials?			

Results Section	Yes/No/Partially	Explanation	Comments/Feedback/ Suggestions
Are the results of the study/experiment clearly stated for *all* tests?			

Figure 6.4 Peer-Review Rubric for Writing in the Sciences *(continued)*

Results Section	Yes/No/Partially	Explanation	Comments/Feedback/Suggestions
Are supporting illustrations, tables, and/or graphs included, with proper captions and in-text references?			
Are explanations and interpretations *withheld* from this section? (Should be in Discussion Section only!)			
Discussion Section	**Yes/No/Partially**	**Explanation**	**Comments/Feedback/Suggestions**
Are the results of the study/experiment clearly summarized at the start of the section?			
Does the author provide explicit explanations and interpretations for the results?			
Are all claims supported with direct references to literature and evidence from the study/experiment?			

Figure 6.4 Peer-Review Rubric for Writing in the Sciences *(continued)*

Discussion Section	Yes/No/Partially	Explanation	Comments/Feedback/ Suggestions
Are in-text citations used correctly to document sources of information and evidence?			
Does the author progress from specific to broad throughout the section (beginning with summary of the current study and ending with overarching themes and applications)?			
Literature Cited Section	**Yes/No/Partially**	**Explanation**	**Comments/Feedback/ Suggestions**
Are all sources used/ cited throughout the text included in the Lit. Cited section?			
Are all sources documented using MLA formatting guidelines, as discussed in class?			

PLC ACTIVITY

Paula adapted peer review to the kind of writing commonly expected in science. With a colleague who does not teach the same subject as you, identify the differences between the more general guidelines for peer review and the guidelines for science writing.

Then, working with a colleague who teaches the same subject as you do, develop guidelines for peer response in the subject you teach.

Notes on College Readiness

One of the habits of mind identified by the "Framework for Success in Postsecondary Writing" is developing flexible writing processes. Here is the way this document describes this habit of mind:

> Writing processes are the multiple strategies writers use to approach and undertake writing and research. Writing processes are not linear. Successful writers use different processes that vary over time and depend on the particular task. For example, a writer may research a topic before drafting, then, after receiving feedback, conduct additional research as part of revising. Writers learn to move back and forth through different stages of writing, adapting those stages to the situation. This ability to employ flexible writing processes is important as students encounter different types of writing tasks that require them to work through the various stages independently to produce final, polished texts.

The Framework goes on to explain what teachers can do to help students develop this habit of mind. Notice the role that peer review plays here.

- Practice all aspects of writing processes including invention, research, drafting, sharing with others, revising in response to reviews, and editing;
- generate ideas and texts using a variety of processes and situate those ideas within different academic disciplines and contexts;
- incorporate evidence and ideas from written, visual, graphic, verbal, and other kinds of texts;
- use feedback to revise texts to make them appropriate for the academic discipline or context for which the writing is intended;

- work with others in various stages of writing; and
- reflect on how different writing tasks and elements of the writing process contribute to their development as a writer.

Occasions for Peer Review

Some teachers think of peer review as appropriate only when students have completed drafts, but it can be equally useful at other times during processes of writing. For example, here are some occasions when peer review can be used:

- during invention or prewriting, when students are generating possibilities for writing
- during early drafting, when students are trying to find their central point
- during later drafting, when students can attend to issues of language and audience
- during revision, when students are dealing with questions about organization and sequence
- during editing, when students are polishing writing by addressing issues of word choice, syntax, and clarity.

Evaluating Plans and Ideas

Early in the process of writing, students can meet to share ideas with other students. Meeting in pairs, students can each, in turn, explain a general plan for writing, including the topic, the main points, and sources of information. In response, partners can do the following:

- Help the writer decide if the topic is too broad or too narrow and offer suggestions for focusing or expanding it.
- Brainstorm at least two details that can be included in the main points.
- Suggest a way to develop the writing.

Evaluating an Early Draft

When students have completed a first draft, they may have written only a few sentences or paragraphs. Still, this can be an excellent time to meet with a group of peers who will share what they have produced. At this stage in the writing process, emphasis still belongs on generating ideas, and discussion with peers can help students learn to evaluate their own plans more effectively. When students are evaluating an early draft, they can do the following:

- Read aloud everything you have written, even if sentences aren't complete. Don't explain what you *meant* to say, just read what's on the paper.
- Ask group members to summarize in one sentence what they heard.
- Based on group response, ask three questions about your draft and write down the responses of each group member.

The process of summarizing someone else's draft helps students develop analytical skills that are essential to becoming better evaluators of their own writing. Asking questions about the responses to their drafts helps authors learn to look at their own work from a slightly distanced perspective, and that ability is key to assessing their own writing.

One of the points of discussion, and sometimes debate, in teacher talk about writing groups is whether group members should have copies of the text or simply listen to the author read aloud. Both procedures are effective, but in the early stages oral reading can prevent students from focusing on surface features like spelling and punctuation at a time when they really need to attend to the overall ideas and shape of the piece. There is plenty of time to turn to surface features when writing is more fully developed.

Evaluating a Later Draft

Once students have found a direction for their writing and have produced several fully developed paragraphs, they are ready to participate in a writing group that attends to issues of language and audience. Of course, attention to audience should begin in the earliest stages of invention and/or prewriting, so that the draft includes appropriate material.

As soon as students start thinking about audience, they begin to focus more closely on their own language. They can start to consider words and phrases in terms of the person who will be reading them. Here, then, is a process that can help students in peer-response writing groups evaluate and revise writing at this stage.

- Before the author starts reading a draft to the group, he or she explains who the audience is.

- Group members list three to five traits they associate with this audience.

- As the author reads the draft aloud, group members note places where the language of the draft is especially well suited to the audience.

- Group members share their notes with the author.

By focusing exclusively on the relationship between audience and language, students develop another evaluative skill. This will help improve their writing in general by enhancing their rhetorical awareness, making them think explicitly about the potential readers of their work. At the same time, it will help them meet the challenges of writing in response to summative assessments by giving them another lens through which they can look at their own writing.

Evaluating for Revisions

When students have been working on a piece of writing for some time, it is often difficult for them to look at their own text with any objectivity. Indeed, we find the same is true for ourselves. After working on multiple drafts, we can no longer remember which sentences are on paper and which are simply inside our heads. When we read the text over, we find ourselves mentally filling in explanations that aren't actually included in the writing. We imagine transitions where none exist, and, unless we read aloud, it's easy to skip over clunky phrasing. These things happen because we read with our brains, not our eyes, and brains fill in what should be on the page and ignore the things that shouldn't be there.

Peer-response writing groups can help writers *see* their own work by providing feedback on drafts. At this point, it is helpful to circulate written texts to group participants before meeting so that everyone can read them in advance. Among the most valuable questions are:

- How would you summarize this selection?

- What parts are unclear?

- Do the parts of this selection seem connected to one another?

- When you get to the end, what questions remain?

Students who answer these questions develop their ability to assess whole pieces of writing, and students who receive answers to these questions get a broader perspective on how readers may respond to their writing. Students are often surprised by what their peers see as the essence of something they have written, and they begin to realize that things they understand completely may not be clear to others. The increased capacity to take the perspective of others, to consider their audience, serves them well as writers because it helps them make the large-scale changes that re-seeing or revising requires.

Evaluating for Polish

If noticing problems in overall structure and wording is difficult for student writers, proofreading the final version for wording choices and conventions of standard written English is *extremely* difficult. Reading the text aloud is one way to find errors because silent readers of their own texts nearly always miss errors. Students can learn to become better proofreaders of their own writing by proofreading the work of their peers. Pairs of students can exchange papers and proofread one another's work. One objection to this practice is that students may not be able to recognize errors or know how to fix them. In our experience, we have found that there are usually a few "grammar nerds" or "spelling champs" in every class, and serving as consultants for their peers gives them an opportunity to shine. Identifying students who can serve as resources for proofreading and encouraging students to pause and ask when they have questions help them learn more about the mechanics of language in an authentic way.

When proofread papers are returned to the original authors, students can do a final exercise to strengthen their ability to evaluate their own work. In addition to correcting their errors, they can analyze them to find out what kinds of mistakes they make most frequently. The error chart shown in Figure 6.5 will help them with this process by asking then to quantify and categorize their errors.

Figure 6.5 Error Chart: Total Number of Errors Identified by the Proofreader

Online 6.8
Error Chart: Total Number of Errors Identified by the Proofreader

Error	Type/Example	How Many
Spelling	Misplaced internal vowel: *wierd* for *weird*	
Spelling	Prefix/suffix: *scarfs* for *scarves*	
Spelling	Pronunciation/structural: *waring* for *wearing*	
Wrong word	*Are* for *our*, *where* for *were*, or *it's* for *its*	
Punctuation	Comma	
Punctuation	Semicolon, colon, or hyphen	
Capitalization	Proper name, sentence beginning	
Usage	Subject-verb agreement: *he don't* for *he doesn't*	
Unintentional sentence fragment	*Running down the street* for *the thief was running down the street*	
Incorrect modifier	*The horse ran quick* for *The horse ran quickly*, or *He took the joke literal* for *He took the joke literally*	
Run-on sentence	*Mary was noisy at first now she's settled down* for *Mary was noisy at first, but now she's settled down*	
Unclear pronoun reference	*Joe called Frank when he got home* for *When he got home, Joe called Frank*	
Misused preposition	*We divided the reward between the four of us* for *We divided the reward among the four of us*	

Self-Evaluation

One central goal of writing instruction is to help students become better evaluators of their own writing. In all writing situations, including writing tests, students need to be able to assess their own writing effectively. The various processes of peer review serve as the best preparation for self-evaluation because in learning to identify problems in the writing of others, students are developing skills they can apply to their own writing. In addition, it is useful for student writers to imagine themselves in the position of an evaluator and have a few processes they can go through to evaluate their own writing. Here are a few possibilities:

- Make an outline of your piece of writing. Include major and minor headings. If you have difficulty finding information to fit into each category, look again at transitions and connecting ideas in your writing.

- Imagine the audience specified by the prompt or assignment, if there is one. List at least five things this audience does. With that mind-set, reread your writing, asking whether it addresses the concerns of the audience.

- Read your work aloud. This will slow you down enough to catch errors that would be difficult to see during silent reading. In a test environment, simply whisper to yourself. Since you won't have time to recopy your work, this is a quick way to eliminate glaring problems.

- Recall the kinds of errors that you have made on other pieces of writing and scan your work for these.

Whether analyzing their own errors, participating in a conference with a teacher, or working through a sequence of formative evaluations, students can improve as writers by participating in multiple forms of assessment. By regularly engaging students in various forms of assessment, especially formative assessment, teachers can help students see how assessment is intimately and positively connected with their capacity to become better writers.

Chapter Seven

The CCSS Performance Task

CHAPTER OVERVIEW *This chapter provides strategies for:*

- *identifying similarities and differences in PARCC and SBAC performance tasks*

- *understanding a SBAC performance task*

- *analyzing prompts*

- *developing rhetorical strategies for writers*

- *comparing generic and assignment specific rubrics*

- *creating effective assignments.*

So what will students actually be asked to do when faced with the writing tasks that are part of the CCSS assessment? Both PARCC and Smarter Balanced Assessment Consortium (SBAC) assessments have two dimensions: an ELA test and an ELA performance task. The term *performance task* is used to designate the portion of the assessment in which students are asked to do extended writing. However, the ELA test also requires that students write short selections. These short selections ask students to do a variety of writing tasks, such as revising provided paragraphs, explaining textual details that support a conclusion, and assessing the effect of stylistic choices in a text. In addition, many of the multiple-choice items call upon writerly understandings, such as identifying the focus of a passage, understanding organizational structures, and discerning how context shapes the meaning of words. Most important, both the ELA test and the ELA performance task emphasize support for claims. In the test, it takes the form of asking students to identify how statements are supported by evidence; in the performance task, students are required to produce evidence-based writing.

To be sure, PARCC and SBAC assessments are not identical. They differ in many ways: the number of grades in which students will be tested (PARCC tests every year in grades 3–11, and SBAC in grades 3–8 and 11); the total amount of time that testing will take (PARCC requires more time for testing at each grade level); the time allowed for the testing window (PARCC allows 4 weeks and SBAC, 12 weeks); as well as other features including cost, teacher role in formative assessment, and achievement-level descriptors. Still, they share many commonalities, including these:

- emphasis on reading substantial texts on which writing tasks are based
- close alignment between CCSS standards and test items
- reading selections that extend from English language arts to science and social studies
- attention to more than one standard in test items
- requirement of multiple genres or modes for student writing
- sequences of questions about the text that precede the prompt for performance tasks.

To prepare students to succeed on these tasks, teachers of all subjects will need to give substantial attention to helping students read strategically. Reading strategically means attending to what point is being made as well as *how* it is being made, what support is offered for a claim, what persuasive strategies an author uses, what special meanings are being conveyed, and what organizational structure is being used. These assessments will also require students to read nonprint forms such as video or websites. In other words, CCSS assessments of writing are as much about reading as they are about writing. This is such a profound shift that we probably should have titled our book *Reading and Writing on Demand*!

SBAC Eighth-Grade Performance Task

Online 7.1
SBAC ELA Grade 8 Performance Task

For an illustration of the kind of reading students will be required to do, consider the sample SBAC performance task for grade 8 that follows. The computer screen is divided in half with the text on the left—where they will have to scroll down to read all three of the selections necessary for completing the assessment—and the questions and text boxes for student writing on the right. A link to this sample item can be found in the online resources.

Part 1

As students scroll down, they are prompted to write brief responses to questions 1 through 3, which follow. Then they are led to collect material for writing, read the assignment, consider the criteria for evaluation, and enact processes of writing.

1. Provide three arguments from the sources you just read that support the position that the penny should be preserved. Be sure to include the titles or numbers of the sources for each argument you provide.

2. Now provide three arguments from the sources that support the position that the penny should be eliminated. Be sure to include the title or the number of the source for each argument you provide.

3. One of the areas of dispute in the argument about whether to keep or get rid of the penny is what will happen to prices of goods. The sources answer this question differently.

    Part A
    Identify one piece of support and the source for the support for the following view: Prices will not go up because of the elimination of the penny.

Students' responses to questions about arguments made in source texts provide them with material to use in the next part of the test.

Part 2

You will now review your sources, take notes, and plan, draft, revise, and edit your essay. You may use your notes and refer to the sources. Now read your assignment and the information about how your argumentative essay will be scored; then begin your work.

Your Assignment

The writing assignment asks students to draw on what they have read in order to produce a persuasive argument.

Now that you have read the sources, you will take a position and present your findings at your school's yearly mock congressional session. For your presentation, analyze the arguments and make a claim about whether or not the penny should be preserved. Make sure you address potential counter-arguments in your essay and support your claim with information from the sources you have examined.

Argumentative Scoring

By providing an indication of how the writing will be scored, the test gives students information about what is expected of them.

Your argumentative essay will be scored using the following:

1. *Statement of claim and organization:* How well did you state your claim, address opposing claims, and maintain your claim with a logical progression of ideas from beginning to end? How well did your idea thoughtfully flow from beginning to end using effective transitions? How effective was your introduction and your conclusion?

2. *Elaboration/evidence:* How well did you integrate relevant and specific information from the sources? How well did you elaborate your ideas? How well did you clearly state ideas using precise language that is appropriate for your audience and purpose?

3. *Conventions:* How well did you follow the rules of grammar usage, punctuation, capitalization, and spelling?

Now Begin Work on Your Argumentative Essay

Notice that students are directed to give attention to aspects of writing processes at the same time that they are reminded of the time limits on their work.

Manage your time carefully so that you can

1. plan your essay,

2. write your essay, and

3. revise and edit the final draft of your essay.

Word-processing tools and spell check are available to you.

For Part 2 you are being asked to write a multi-paragraph essay, so please be as thorough as possible. Type your response in the space provided. The box will expand as you type. Remember to check your notes and your prewriting/planning.

As this sample makes clear, students will have to gather information from a given text to do the extended writing required in the performance task. Questions like 1–3 in Part 1 make it essential for them to read carefully and gather details that they can use in providing evidence to support the claims they make in writing in response to the prompt in Part 2. Indeed, the version of this item that we reviewed did not allow students to leave the screen with questions 1–3 of Part 1 without answering each question. Students may need help to understand the relationship between sections like Part 1 and Part 2. In the version we reviewed there were no instructions about how to access the information from Part 1 when writing Part 2 even though the directions for Part 2 include a reminder to "check your notes." Even if the instructions were clear, students might still need practice in reading selections on multiple subjects and identifying the evidence used to support claims made.

Another feature of the instructions for Part 2, the SBAC extended writing prompt, is this list:

> *Now begin work on your argumentative essay.*
> Manage your time carefully so that you can
>
> 1. plan your essay
>
> 2. write your essay
>
> 3. revise and edit the final draft of your essay.
>
> Word-processing tools and spell check are available to you.

Even though this assessment provides limited time for students to write in response to the prompt, it provides a clear directive that students should use processes of writing in responding to the assessment. It is easy for students to assume that the best way to approach any high-stakes writing prompt is by just starting to write as quickly as possible. The directions above are a useful antidote to this impulse, but even when such directions are not provided, students need to know their work will be improved by treating even timed writing as an occasion for process writing. Chapter 8 will deal in more detail with strategies for using writing processes in timed writing, but the first step is recognizing the importance of doing so.

Teachers can help students with this SBAC prompt by giving them opportunities to practice strategic reading. Here, for example, is an excerpt from *Narrative of the Life of Frederick Douglass, an American Slave* that students in social studies or English might be expected to read.

> The plan which I adopted, and the one by which I was most successful, was that of making friends of all the little white boys whom I met in the street. As many of these as I could, I converted into teachers. With their kindly aid, obtained at different times and in different places, I finally succeeded in learning to read. When I was sent on errands, I always took my book with

me, and by going one part of my errand quickly, I found time to get a lesson before my return. I used also to carry bread with me, enough of which was always in the house, and to which I was always welcome; for I was much better off in this regard than many of the poor white children in our neighborhood. This bread I used to bestow upon the hungry little urchins, who, in return, would give me that more valuable bread of knowledge. I am strongly tempted to give the names of two or three of those little boys, as a testimonial of the gratitude and affection I bear them; but prudence forbids;—not that it would injure me, but it might embarrass them; for it is almost an unpardonable offence to teach slaves to read in this Christian country. It is enough to say of the dear little fellows, that they lived on Philpot Street, very near Durgin and Bailey's ship-yard. I used to talk this matter of slavery over with them. I would sometimes say to them, I wished I could be as free as they would be when they got to be men. "You will be free as soon as you are twenty-one, but I am a slave for life! Have not I as good a right to be free as you have?" These words used to trouble them; they would express for me the liveliest sympathy, and console me with the hope that something would occur by which I might be free.

I was now about twelve years old, and the thought of being a slave for life began to bear heavily upon my heart. Just about this time, I got hold of a book entitled "The Columbian Orator." Every opportunity I got, I used to read this book. Among much of other interesting matter, I found in it a dialogue between a master and his slave. The slave was represented as having run away from his master three times. The dialogue represented the conversation which took place between them, when the slave was retaken the third time. In this dialogue, the whole argument in behalf of slavery was brought forward by the master, all of which was disposed of by the slave. The slave was made to say some very smart as well as impressive things in reply to his master—things which had the desired though unexpected effect; for the conversation resulted in the voluntary emancipation of the slave on the part of the master.

In the same book, I met with one of Sheridan's mighty speeches on and in behalf of Catholic emancipation. These were choice documents to me. I read them over and over again with unabated interest. They gave tongue to interesting thoughts of my own soul, which had frequently flashed through my mind, and died away for want of utterance. The moral which I gained from the dialogue was the power of truth over the conscience of even a slaveholder. What I got from Sheridan was a bold denunciation of slavery, and a powerful vindication of human rights. The reading of these documents enabled me to utter my thoughts, and to meet the arguments brought forward to sustain slavery; but while they relieved me of one difficulty, they brought on another even more painful than the one of which I was relieved. The more I read, the more I was led to abhor and detest my enslavers. I could regard them in no other light than a band of successful robbers, who had left their homes, and gone to Africa, and stolen us from our homes, and in a strange land reduced us to slavery. I loathed them as being the meanest as well as the most wicked of men. As I read and contemplated the subject, behold! that very discontentment which Master Hugh had predicted would follow my learning to read had already come, to torment and sting my soul to unutterable anguish. As I writhed under it, I would at times feel that learning to read had been a curse rather than a blessing. It had given me a view of my wretched condition, without the remedy. It opened my eyes to the horrible pit, but to no ladder upon which to get out. In moments of agony, I envied my fellow-slaves for their stupidity. I have often wished myself a beast. I preferred the condition of the meanest reptile to my own. Any thing, no matter what, to get rid of thinking! It was this ever-lasting thinking of my condition that tormented me. There was no getting rid of it. It was pressed upon me by every object within sight or hearing, animate or inanimate. The silver trump of freedom had roused my soul to eternal wakefulness. Freedom now appeared, to disappear no more forever. It was heard in every sound, and seen in every thing. It was ever present to torment me with a sense of my wretched condition. I saw nothing without seeing it, I heard nothing without hearing it, and felt nothing without feeling it. It looked from every star, it smiled in every calm, breathed in every wind, and moved in every storm. (Douglass 1845, 40–42)

The following questions could be used to help students learn to read more strategically.

1. "As I read and contemplated the subject, behold! that very discontentment which Master Hugh had predicted would follow my learning to read had already come, to torment and sting my soul to unutterable anguish." Identify at least two sentences that support the claim made in the sentence above.

2. Douglass uses metaphor to strengthen his argument. Identify one metaphor in this selection and explain its effect.

3. Douglass calls on the strategy of comparison and contrast several times. Select one instance and explain how it supports Douglass's argument about the need to abolish slavery.

One of the most effective ways to develop instructional approaches that will support students' development as readers is to collaborate with colleagues. The following PLC activity suggests ways of beginning this process.

PLC ACTIVITY

Ask members of the PLC who represent different subjects to bring selections that students might be expected to read in their classes.

All members of the team can work together to develop questions that will help students identify the key points in each selection, comparing how this process differs across the disciplines.

Recall the PLC activity from Chapter 1 in which we analyzed the cognitive levels of the Common Core State Standards. This analysis suggests that the kinds of questions we develop should be at the higher levels of Bloom's taxonomy, questions that require students to analyze, compare, assess, summarize, infer, and so forth.

The directions for Part 2 include a considerable amount of information, and students will need help unpacking all of it. To begin, let's consider the "Your Assignment" section since it gives students explicit instructions for writing.

Your Assignment: Now that you have read the sources, you will take a position and present your findings at your school's yearly mock congressional session. For your presentation, analyze the arguments and make a claim as to whether or not the penny should be preserved. Make sure you address potential counterarguments in your essay and support your claim with information from the sources you have examined.

Strategies of prompt analysis can be helpful in preparing students for assessments like these. More importantly, though, learning strategies for prompt analysis can help students with writing in many different contexts, whether an assignment for a class or a writing task in the world of work. Prompt analysis is based on principles of rhetoric that are central in all writing and reading because rhetoric emphasizes identifying central concepts, purpose,

Figure 7.1 Rhetorical Features of the Prompt

Central Claim/ Topic	Audience	Purpose/Mode	Strategies	Role
Preservation of the penny	School's mock congressional session	Argue whether or not penny should be preserved	Supporting evidence, counterarguments	Presenter at mock congress

strategies, and audience. The chart in Figure 7.1 identifies the rhetorical features that are present in the prompt for Part 2.

As this figure shows, rhetoric offers resources students can call upon to complete any piece of writing. By filling in the cells of a chart like this, they answer a number of questions, and answering questions like these will help them become effective readers of whatever writing assignments they face. Of course, writing situations vary widely, and it may not be possible to answer every question in all circumstances. In much school writing, for example, audience is not always specified. However, learning to ask and answer questions about the claim or topic, audience, purpose or mode, strategies, and role of the writer enables students to discern what is required of them and generate ideas for meeting that requirement.

Prompt Analysis Questions

The prompt analysis questions that follow provide an amplified version of these rhetorical questions. These elaborations have proved useful in helping students understand in more detail what and how they are being expected to write.

1. What is the *central claim/topic* called for?
   Do I have choices to make with regard to this claim/topic? Will I need to focus the claim/topic to write a good essay? What arguments can I make for this claim? What do I know about this topic?

2. Who is the intended *audience*?
   If named specifically, what do I know about this particular audience? If the audience is implied or not identified, what can I infer about it or them? In either event, how might the expectations of this audience affect my choices as a writer?

3. What is the *purpose/mode* for the writing task?

   Is the purpose stated or must it be inferred? What is this writing supposed to accomplish (besides fulfilling the demands of the prompt/assignment)? What does the goal of this writing suggest about the mode (narration, exposition, description, argument) or combination of modes that I should consider in responding?

4. What *strategies* will be most effective?

   What does the purpose/mode suggest about possible strategies? Of the strategies I am comfortable using—such as examples, definitions, analysis, classification, cause/effect, compare/contrast—which will be most effective here? Are there any strategies—such as number of examples or type of support—that are specified as required?

Online 7.2
Prompt Analysis Questions

5. What is my *role* as a writer in achieving the purpose?

   Have I been assigned a specific role, like *applicant* or *representative*? If I have not been assigned a specific role, what does the prompt or assignment tell me about the level of expertise I should demonstrate, the stance I should assume, or the approach I should take?

Students will need some help in learning to use these questions effectively. For example, the terms *claim* and *topic* will probably need some clarification. In the SBAC prompt above, the topic is the penny, but the claim focuses on whether the penny should continue to exist. In our experience, some students confuse topic with claim and, faced with this prompt, might assume that it would be satisfactory to write about the penny without taking a position on its continued existence. Similarly, students may need to learn to distinguish between *purpose* and *mode*. In the prompt about the penny, the purpose—to argue that the penny should or should not continue to exist—is directly linked to the mode of argument, but this is not always the case. Some writing assignments specify a mode such as narrative even when the purpose is to make an argument. Furthermore, modes blur into one another given that it's very difficult to write an explanation without some description or an argument without some explanation.

One of the most challenging things for many student writers is understanding different audiences. As we noted in Chapter 6, one of the many advantages of peer review writing groups is that students begin to develop an understanding of audience by getting feedback from multiple peers. The SBAC prompt provides a clear audience—the school's mock congressional session—but many writing assignments indicate no audience, and part of analyzing a prompt is imagining an audience. When no audience is specified in school writing, students usually assume that the audience is the teacher, and even this

Figure 7.2 Rhetorical Strategies

Online 7.3
*Rhetorical
Strategies*

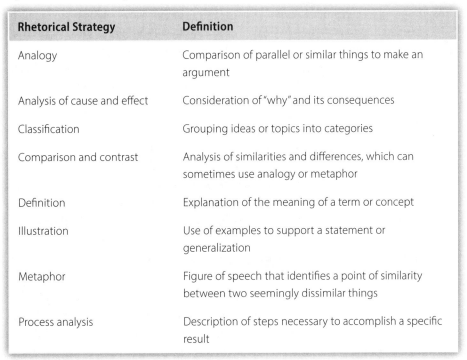

Rhetorical Strategy	Definition
Analogy	Comparison of parallel or similar things to make an argument
Analysis of cause and effect	Consideration of "why" and its consequences
Classification	Grouping ideas or topics into categories
Comparison and contrast	Analysis of similarities and differences, which can sometimes use analogy or metaphor
Definition	Explanation of the meaning of a term or concept
Illustration	Use of examples to support a statement or generalization
Metaphor	Figure of speech that identifies a point of similarity between two seemingly dissimilar things
Process analysis	Description of steps necessary to accomplish a specific result

audience can be analyzed to guide writing. Students can assume, for instance, that teachers are adults who will expect a relatively formal style and details to support claims made. They might also assume, based on the subject area, something about which specialized terms or key concepts should be included.

Students will also need help understanding the strategies they might consider in analyzing a writing prompt. In instructing students to use supporting evidence and make a counter argument, the language of the SBAC prompt specifies strategies that students should use in completing the prompt, but many writing assignments do not include this level of detail. Some prompts will do the equivalent of simply telling students to argue for or against the continuation of the penny, and students will need to decide for themselves what strategies to use. One way to prepare students for determining what strategies to use is to spend time considering various rhetorical strategies; Figure 7.2 shows some of the most common strategies. By giving students opportunities to explore how these strategies work, they can increase their repertoire of ways to analyze and respond to prompts and assignments.

Still another area where students will need help is the category of role or stance. The SBAC prompt provides student writers with a clear role—presenter at the school's mock congress—and that role implies that writers will take an authoritative stance, displaying knowledge of the subject and making a convincing argument. In many cases, however, no role is assigned, and students need to determine for themselves what stance to take. Of course, when an audience is specified, it is much easier for students to decide on a stance.

Notes on College Readiness

Rhetoric is a term that is often used negatively, as in "that's just rhetoric." For writing teachers, however, rhetoric is foundational. Many of the terms and processes used in writing instruction have their origins in Aristotle's *Rhetoric* or other studies of rhetoric. For example, *prewriting*, a term often used to describe early stages of writing, is a version of what Aristotle called *invention*. In Aristotle's terms, invention was the process of discovering all the possible arguments. Today's writing teachers may ask students to map, free write, brainstorm, or list evidence in order to make an argument.

Prompt analysis is grounded in the rhetorical triangle of audience, purpose, and subject. It recognizes that writers always work in a rhetorical context and aims to help students develop strategies for responding effectively to prompts in a variety of contexts. This skill is essential for college readiness. The "Framework for Success in Postsecondary Writing" includes the following in its list of what is essential for college writing:

> Rhetorical knowledge—the ability to analyze and act on understandings of audiences, purposes, and contexts in creating and comprehending texts

> Rhetorical knowledge is the basis of good writing. By developing rhetorical knowledge, writers can adapt to different purposes, audiences, and contexts. Study of and practice with basic rhetorical concepts, such as purpose, audience, context, and conventions, are important as writers learn to compose a variety of texts for different disciplines and purposes. For example, a writer might draft one version of a text with one audience in mind and then revise the text to meet the needs and expectations of a different audience.

Just as students can benefit from practice with strategic reading, so they can benefit from opportunities to analyze prompts. In preparation for leading prompt analysis with students, teachers may find it helpful to analyze prompts with colleagues.

PLC ACTIVITY

Select writing prompts that might be used in your discipline; then, in your PLC group, use the prompt analysis questions to unpack what is required by prompts in various subjects. Alternatively, analyze the prompts included here.

PARCC 11–12 Prompt

Compare two or more recorded or live productions of Arthur Miller's *Death of a Salesman* to the written text, evaluating how each version interprets the source text and debating which aspects of the enacted interpretations of the play best capture a particular character, scene, or theme.

PARCC 9–10 Prompt

Analyze how Abraham Lincoln in his Second Inaugural Address examines the ideas that led to the Civil War, paying particular attention to the order in which the points are made, how Lincoln introduces and develops his points, and the connections that are drawn among them.

PARCC 11–12 Prompt

Use what you have learned from reading "Daedalus and Icarus" by Ovid and "To a Friend Whose Work Has Come to Triumph" by Anne Sexton to write an essay that provides an analysis of how Sexton transforms Daedalus and Icarus.

As a starting point, you may want to consider what is emphasized, absent, or different in the two texts, but feel free to develop your own focus for analysis.

Develop your essay by providing textual evidence from both texts. Be sure to follow the conventions of standard English.

Criteria for Evaluation

The SBAC prompt is followed by an explanation of the criteria that will be used to evaluate the writing produced by the student.

Argumentative Scoring

Your argumentative essay will be scored using the following:

1. *Statement of claim and organization*: How well did you state your claim, address opposing claims, and maintain your claim with a logical progression of ideas from beginning to end? How well did your idea thoughtfully flow from beginning to end using effective transitions? How effective was your introduction and your conclusion?

2. *Elaboration/evidence:* How well did you integrate relevant and specific information from the sources? How well did you elaborate your ideas? How well did you clearly state ideas using precise language that is appropriate for your audience and purpose?

3. *Conventions:* How well did you follow the rules of grammar usage, punctuation, capitalization, and spelling?

Just as it is helpful to teach students how to analyze prompts, it is valuable to show them how to unpack a rubric or list of criteria for evaluation. Whether for a CCSS assessment or any other writing project, students benefit from knowing what is expected of them, and the criteria for evaluation are among the most explicit statements of expectations.

One important thing students need to understand about rubrics is that some are generic and some are assignment specific. The rubric for the SBAC performance task is generic; it can be used with a variety of other tasks that ask for an argumentative essay. Likewise, the language about the flow of ideas, effective introduction and conclusion, integrating information, elaborating ideas, using precise language, and following conventions could be applied to many writing assignments.

Another feature of this SBAC rubric is that while it appears to have three main criteria, it actually includes five different criteria. Making a claim is not the same as organizing a piece of writing, and including evidence is different from elaborating ideas. To be sure, good organization can make the terms of a claim more effective, and including evidence to support a claim may contribute to the elaboration of ideas, but it is not the same thing. Students will benefit from opportunities to examine the parts of rubrics so that they can respond to them most effectively.

Classroom Moves

Ask students to look at the generic rubric shown in Figure 7.3 and describe in their own words what would be different between a piece of writing that receives all 4's and one that receives all 1's.

Online 7.4
Generic Rubric

Figure 7.3 Generic Rubric

Score	4	3	2	1
Ideas/content	Essay has a clear focus, ideas are compelling, there is good development and strong support.	Focus is apparent, some development takes place, and ideas offer support, though it may not be consistent.	Focus is not clear, ideas need development, and/or more support is needed for ideas.	No focus, lack of development and/or support may be unacceptably brief.
Organization	Introduction includes a strong thesis, clear topic sentences, smooth transitions between ideas, and strong closure.	Clear introduction, body, and conclusions, although transitions could be smoother.	Lapses in organization begin to detract from the meaning of the essay.	Organization is unclear or essay consists of one long paragraph with no sorting and grouping of ideas.
Voice/word choice	Voice sounds like an individual, with consistency throughout the piece; word choice is precise and sophisticated.	Voice is good, though not superlative; words are correct and sufficient to convey meaning.	Voice is inconsistent; word choice is not always correct.	Voice may be inappropriate; words are carelessly chosen or just plain wrong.

Figure 7.3 Generic Rubric *(continued)*

Score	4	3	2	1
Sentence structure/ writing conventions	Sentence structure is correct and varied; few, if any, grammar errors.	Sentence structure is generally correct, though not as varied as it could be; some grammar errors.	Sentence structure errors require frequent rereading; grammar errors begin to impede meaning.	Poor sentence structure; many grammar errors.

When students have finished speculating about the differences between a 4 and a 1 paper according to this rubric, show them the assignment-specific rubrics in Figure 7.4 and ask them to compare it with the generic one. This rubric was created by Sarah Guzick, a science teacher, whose assignment asked students to create a travel brochure describing the biome they had been studying. Sarah divided this rubric into five sections, each focused on a specific part of the travel brochure. Figure 7.4 covers the basic information of the brochure. Figure 7.5 is about the activities that can be done in the biome. The weather section is evaluated using the part of the rubric in Figure 7.6. Threats to the biome are evaluated in Figure 7.7, and Figure 7.8 provides criteria for the analysis of the biome.

Figure 7.4 Assignment-Specific Rubric—Basic Information

4	3	2	1
Biome's location correctly and clearly identified (should contain text and a map)	Correct location and no visual *or* visual and incorrect location	Incorrectly located and no visual	No biome location and no visual
Three abiotic factors identified and described	Two abiotic factors identified and described	One abiotic factor identified and described	No abiotic factors listed/described

Figure 7.4 Assignment-Specific Rubric—Basic Information *(continued)*

4	3	2	1
Two native plants indicated	Two plants indicated but only one is native	One native plant included	No plants included *or* none are native
Adaptations given for all native plants	Adaptations provided for one plant	Incorrect adaptations provided for plants	No adaptations provided
Two native animals indicated	Two animals indicated but only one is native	One native animal included	No plants included *or* none are native
Adaptations given for all native animals	Adaptations provided for one animal	Incorrect adaptations provided for animals	No adaptations provided
Two examples of cooperation and/or competition provided with description	One example of cooperation and/or competition with no description	One example of cooperation and/or competition with no description	No examples

Figure 7.5 What Can Be Done There?

4	3	2	1
Three recreational activities listed	Two recreational activities listed	One recreational activity listed	No recreational activities listed
Two points of interest listed and described	One point of interest noted and described	One or two points of interest noted with no description	No points of interest represented
Two nearby biomes correctly identified	One other biome identified that is nearby	Two other biomes identified but not nearby	One other biome identified but not nearby

Figure 7.6 Weather Report

4	3	2	1
Average precipitation correct and clearly indicated	Correct but not clearly indicated	Incorrect but clearly indicated	No information given
Average temperature correct and clearly indicated	Correct but not clearly indicated	Incorrect but clearly indicated	No information given
Suggested supplies, gear, clothing, etc., included	Addresses only some of the listed items	Addresses only one of the listed items	No suggestions given

Figure 7.7 Warnings

4	3	2	1
Threats to biome identified and described	Adequately identified; little or no description/discussion	Not well identified; little or no description	Threats not identified
Three endangered species identified (with pictures)	Two species identified (with pictures)	One or two endangered species identified; no pictures	No endangered species identified
Impact of climate change completely addressed	Impact adequately addressed	Impact minimally addressed	Impact not addressed

Figure 7.8 Analysis/Evaluation

4	3	2	1
Explanation of global importance reasonable and understandable	Explanation reasonable but not clearly understood	Explanation understandable but not reasonable	Global importance not explained

A PARCC Performance Task

Here is a writing task produced by the PARCC consortium. It is based on three texts about Amelia Earhart, which students read to prepare for writing. There are three parts to this performance task.

Part 1 of 7th grade PARCC Performance Task

This first part asks students to focus on one aspect of Earhart's life.

> Question: Based on the information in the text "Biography of Amelia Earhart," write an essay that summarizes and explains the challenges Earhart faced throughout her life. Remember to use textual evidence to support your ideas.

Part 2 of 7th grade PARCC Performance Task

In this part students are asked to show their ability to read carefully and accurately.

> Below are three claims that one could make based on the article "Earhart's Final Resting Place Believed Found."
>
> - Earhart and Noonan lived as castaways on Nikumaroro Island.
> - Earhart and Noonan's plane crashed into the Pacific Ocean.
> - People don't really know where Earhart and Noonan died.

Part A

Highlight the claim that is supported by the most relevant and sufficient evidence within "Earhart's Final Resting Place Believed Found."

Part B

Click on two facts within the article that best provide evidence to support the claim selected in Part A.

Like the SBAC performance task, this one requires students to read strategically to gather information. When they have completed this section, students turn to the part that requires more extended writing.

Part 3 of 7th grade PARCC Performance Task

This part of the test requires students to draw on multiple texts to make an argument.

Constructed Response from Research Simulation Task (analytical essay)

You have read three texts describing Amelia Earhart. All three include the claim that Earhart was a brave, courageous person. The three texts are:

- "Biography of Amelia Earhart"

- "Earhart's Final Resting Place Believed Found"

- "Amelia Earhart's Life and Disappearance"

Consider the argument each author uses to demonstrate Earhart's bravery.

Write an essay that analyzes the strength of the arguments about Earhart's bravery in at least two of the texts. Remember to use textual evidence to support your ideas.

This prompt does not include the directions for writing or the criteria for evaluation that were included in the SBAC prompt. PARCC does, however, have a generic rubric that includes these criteria: (1) development of ideas, (2) organization, (3) clarity of language, and (4) conventions.

Here is a response to Part 1 of this task written by Odetta, a seventh grader, at the beginning of the school year:

Amelia Earhart

The challenges of Amelia Earhart were devastating. When she was flying across the Atlantic Ocean the winds were tribally icy. Also, there were mechanical problems. When she was breaking other records, she had to be rescued from a crowed that overflowed the field by husky policemen. Earhart wanted to be the first woman to fly around the world, but she was almost 40 and her plane was damaged. While Amelia and her navigator were flying around the world their maps were inaccurate. They were trying to find Howland but it's a small spot and they couldn't see it. The weather reports were favorable but there were rain showers. The rain made it difficult to navigate. The clouds didn't help either. Earhart's radio was irregular through most of the flight. It was always being interrupted by static. She had many challenges in her life but when her fuel ran out and her plane crashed was probally the most devastating one.

After reading this essay and many others like it, Odetta's teacher, Alissa Helm, was concerned that her students would not be able to succeed on CCSS assessments. However, Alissa decided that a rich diet of literacy could enable her students to improve their reading and writing. Accordingly, she launched a program of instruction that included the following approach to writing (see Chapter 3 for a more detailed explanation of Levels 1–3):

Level 1 writing (ungraded writing for the self):

- Daily writing
- Use of graphic organizers, free-writes
- High interest prompts that relate to literacy activities
- Writing to learn

Level 2 writing (drafts directed to an audience but not yet polished):

- Practice summarization
- Book reflections—summary plus three paragraphs of reflection
- Silent literature circles
- Practice using textual evidence

Level 3 writing (polished writing ready for scrutiny by an audience):

- Storyboard fables
- Persuasive writing—formulate a persuasive letter (authentic) with support

Near the end of the school year, Alissa asked her students to respond to the following prompt, based on the Amelia Earhart PARCC prompt:

> Based on the information in the text "Biography of Sarah Winnemucca," write an essay that *summarizes* and *explains* the *challenges* Winnemucca faced throughout her life. Remember to use *text evidence* to support your ideas.

Here is the essay Odetta wrote:

Challenges of Sarah Winnemucca

Sarah Winnemucca had several Challenges in her life. They started when she was very little when the white people first came. The white people burned their whole food supplies for the winter. Also, Sarah's mother buried her and her cousins so the white people couldn't find them. That made her afraid of white people.

When Sarah was younger there was no school for Indian children so she went to school at Ormsby's house with his daughter. After that she went to a boarding school for a while. Then the white kid's parents didn't like her there so she got kicked out.

In the time period 1860–1878 two wars broke out The Pyramid Lake War, which Sarah's grandfather died, and the Bannock War. In the Bannock War Sarah was hired as a translator for the U.S. Government. She had to go back and forth between the two tribes, while at risk of getting hurt in different ways. Also, she had trouble negotiation with the different sides. Sarah's tribe got mad at her when she translated things they didn't actually say.

After the war, Sarah's tribe was forced to leave their home and go to the Yakima Indian Reservation. Their life was harsh on the reservation. The government kept steeling their food and clothes that were meant for them. Also, the weather and living conditions where horrible. A long time after that, Sarah returned home and she opened a school for Indian children. A lot of people criticized her school but it was very successful.

Sarah's tribe became ill with a disease that the European settlers brought with them. Awhile after her tribe got sick, she did too. Sarah moved in with her sister in her home in Monida, Montana. Then she died on October 17th, 1891. Sarah's life was complicated and harsh, but she got through it. She was a very dedicated to her work and what she did in her life.

Alissa's other students showed similar improvement in synthesizing information from the article, referring to more than one challenge and organizing their ideas into a coherent whole. This experience convinced her that while it is not necessary to teach to the test, students do need explicit instruction in using textual evidence effectively in their own writing. She also learned that students benefit from opportunities to talk about their own processes so that they develop a metacognitive understanding of how they write. The biography of Sarah Winnemucca can be found in the online materials.

Online 7.6
Biography of Sarah Winnemucca

RESEARCH AND POLITICAL CONSIDERATIONS

Although rubrics and criteria for evaluation have been released by PARCC and SBAC, the actual method by which extended writing will be assessed remains unclear. One approach that has been discussed is machine scoring, a process by which computers would "read" student texts. Not surprisingly, this possibility has raised concern among many teachers, and in April of 2013, the National Council of Teachers issued its Position Statement on Machine Scoring. It can be found in our online materials.

Online 7.7
Position Statement on Machine Scoring

This statement is worth reading because it brings together insights from classrooms, research, and advocacy groups such as the Professionals against Machine Scoring of Student Essays in High-Stakes Assessment Petition Initiative. A description of this group can be found in our online materials.

Online 7.8
Professionals Against Machine Scoring of Student Essays

The issues raised in this document merit discussion with students, parents, administrators, and community members.

Creating Effective Assignments

One of the things we have learned from our own experience analyzing prompts and rubrics is that both are very useful for the *creation* of assignments. We have come to understand that the typical student question, "What do you want?" usually indicates that we have not done an adequate job of making the topic or claim, audience, purpose or mode strategies, and role clear enough for students to know how to proceed in their responses. Accordingly, we often use the prompt analysis questions as a lens through which we can examine the assignments given to our students. Likewise, we find that creating a rubric, either with student involvement or to let students see it while they are writing, helps us—and our students—understand the assignment more clearly.

Producing assignments that can stand up to rhetorical questions and creating rubrics to go with assignments takes time, but by doing so we get fewer questions from perplexed students. Better yet, we see improved student writing when we craft our assignments carefully and create rubrics to go with them. And in a world where concerns about plagiarism abound, we find that students cannot buy or download writing that responds to carefully crafted assignments.

PLC ACTIVITY

Ask someone in the group to bring a writing assignment to a PLC meeting.

Using the prompt analysis questions discussed in this chapter, suggest ways of making individual assignments easier for students to understand.

As a group, develop a rubric for the assignment.

Even with the best prompts, even when rubrics are included, even when students are encouraged to use process writing, producing an effective piece of writing can be challenging in a timed-writing context. The next chapter offers strategies for meeting this challenge.

Chapter Eight

Writing (and Reading) in Time

CHAPTER OVERVIEW *This chapter provides strategies for:*

● *analyzing SBAC and PARCC assessment contexts*

● *analyzing prompts*

● *building on student facility with writing on demand using social media*

● *making the big shift from writing on demand to reading and writing on demand*

● *managing time in a digital space.*

Time is the dimension that makes writing on demand different from other kinds of writing we do. Time is objective—students have a finite number of minutes in which to write. However, time is also subjective. Our perception of time can be altered dramatically by our feelings. For example, the emotion of fear causes us to overestimate how much time had passed. Perhaps this is why in a life-or-death situation, so many people report, "I saw my life flash before my eyes" or why in a car crash people say that time seems to slow down.

Understanding of time is also developmental. A child's awareness of time improves as the prefrontal cortex develops. It is important for teachers to know that "time estimation is impaired in students with Attention Deficit Hyperactivity Disorder" (Toplak et al. 2006). Therefore, we need to work explicitly with all students on how to manage time in a testing situation.

Students need to have a sense of time to successfully plan, write, and revise an essay, and emotions, memory, and attention all affect an individual's perception of time. Furthermore, emotional responses to testing situations vary widely among students, and this

157

needs to be addressed. We recommend that student fears be faced and discussed. Again, metacognitive strategies are key in reflecting on how the mind is working in timed testing situations and in helping students develop an individual "game plan" for how to function well in these situations.

The best place to start is the context of the test itself. Students can learn to develop game plans when they understand what is expected of them.

Analysis of SBAC and PARCC Assessment Contexts

Before starting any writing-on-demand task, teachers can help students demystify the writing task by asking the following context analysis questions.

Five Key Context Analysis Questions

1. What is my time limit?

2. What kinds of writing aids are available to me? Is there, for example, a writing checklist, a rubric, and so on?

3. What are the targeted skills? What particular thinking or writing skills does this test require? What standards are being assessed?

4. What kind of format is expected? Will a five-paragraph essay work here or is some other format required?

5. What specialized expectations are implicit in this particular writing task? For example, is length or audience specified?

Online 8.1
Five Key Context Analysis Questions

Smarter Balanced Performance Task

The Smarter Balanced Performance Task (SBAC) for eleventh grade is designed to take 120 minutes total, far longer than most previous on-demand writing tests, like the ACT (30 minutes). The creators of the SBAC provide the following time allotments for these parts of the test:

(20 minutes) *Classroom Activity.* In this part, the teacher activates student prior knowledge about the topic through discussion and assures that all students know the definitions or basic concepts that are prelude to success on the test.

For example, in the Nuclear Power sample found online, the teacher makes sure students understand that nuclear power is one of several ways that societies produce energy and that there is controversy about its use.

Online 8.2
SBAC 11th Grade Performance Task on Nuclear Power

(50 minutes) *Part 1—Reading.* Students read source texts on the topic. They are guided to demonstrate understanding of core concepts by answering constructed-response questions on the topic. Students can take notes on the source texts and use them in the next section.

(70 minutes) *Part 2—Writing.* Students write an argument using the source texts. Students are responsible for planning their prewriting, drafting, and revising. It is this last part in which students will need to work independently, using their sense of time. We recommend the breakdown of the 70 minutes that is shown in the next section, but students should do what works best for them.

Planning to Use Time in a Writing Test

1. Note how long you have to complete the writing selection.

2. Look at the clock and write what you see in Figure 8.1 on a piece of paper.

Figure 8.1 Allocating Time in a Writing Test

Online 8.3
Allocating Time in a Writing Test

Directions for Allocating Time	Example with the SBAC (70 min.)	Process of Writing on Demand
Time the writing test begins: _____	1:00 p.m.	Allocate your time.
Time that marks one-quarter of the available minutes: _____	1:18 p.m. (70 min × .25 = 17.5, rounded up to 18)	Plan your essay (18 min.). 1:00–1:18 p.m.
Time that marks three-quarters of the available minutes: _____	1:53 p.m. (70 min × .75 = 52.5, rounded up to 53)	Write your essay (35 min.). 1:18–1:53 p.m.
Time the writing test ends: _____	2:10 p.m.	Revise your essay (17 min.). 1:53–2:10 p.m.

3. Use the first quarter of the available time to plan your writing. In the example in Figure 8.1, this means that from 1:00–1:18 you should be planning. This includes carefully reading and analyzing the prompt, answering the context analysis questions, prewriting, and developing a thesis or controlling idea.

4. When the clock indicates that a quarter of the time has elapsed, consider where you are in the planning process. If necessary, you can take a few more minutes to prepare your plan, but in the example in Figure 8.1, you would be drafting from 1:18–1:53 p.m. (about 35 minutes).

5. As you write, glance at the clock occasionally, and keep looking at your thesis and prewriting to keep them in the forefront of your mind.

6. One-quarter minutes before the end of the allotted time, draw your writing to a close, stop, and take a breath. Prepare your mind to move from drafting to revising.

7. In the last quarter of time, reread and revise as necessary. In the example in the figure, the time from 1:53 to 2:10 would be devoted to revision. Revision will necessarily be limited to small changes like adding a sentence or two to strengthen your ideas or make a transition, deleting repeated or unnecessary words, adding more precise or vivid vocabulary, correcting mistakes, adding missed punctuation, and so forth. You can also consider the organization of the whole piece and decide whether a different order of paragraphs would be better.

PARCC Performance Task

Here is a tenth-grade test item released by PARCC.

Sample Literary Analysis Item for Grade 10

Online 8.4
"Daedalus and Icarus"

Students begin by reading an excerpt from Ovid titled "Daedalus and Icarus." Here are the first eight lines of the excerpt, which is 110 lines long. The full text can be found in online resources.

> But Daedalus abhorred the Isle of Crete—
> and his long exile on that sea-girt shore,
> increased the love of his own native place.
> "Though Minos blocks escape by sea and land."
> He said, "The unconfined skies remain

though Minos may be lord of all the world
his sceptre is not regnant of the air,
and by that untried way is our escape."

After reading the excerpt, students answer the multiple-choice questions in Parts 1 and 2. At some point prior to writing the essay, students are also to read a poem by Anne Sexton "To a Friend Whose Work Has Come to Triumph," which is a sonnet (14 lines) that refers to Icarus and Daedalus.

Part 1

The questions in this section ask students to interpret Ovid's poem and identify sections of the text to justify their views. Note that it is necessary to get the first question right in order to succeed on the second. This is characteristic of all the PARCC selected-response items we have reviewed.

1. Which of the following sentences best states an important theme about human behavior as described in Ovid's "Daedalus and Icarus"?

    a. Striving to achieve one's dreams is a worthwhile endeavor.

    b. The thoughtlessness of youth can have tragic results.

    c. Imagination and creativity bring their own rewards.

    d. Everyone should learn from his or her mistakes.

2. Select three pieces of evidence from Ovid's "Daedalus and Icarus" that support the answer to Part 1.

    a. "and by his playfulness retard the work/his anxious father planned" (lines 310–311).

    b. "But when at last/the father finished it, he poised himself" (lines 312–313).

    c. "he fitted on his son the plumed wings/ with trembling hands, while down his withered cheeks/the tears were falling" (lines 327–329).

    d. "Proud of his success/the foolish Icarus forsook his guide" (lines 348–349).

    e. "and, bold in vanity, began to soar/rising upon his wings to touch the skies" (lines 350–351).

    f. "and as the years went by the gifted youth/began to rival his instructor's art" (lines 376–377).

g. "Wherefore Daedalus/enraged and envious, sought to slay the youth" (lines 384–385).

h. "The Partridge hides/in shaded places by the leafy trees ... for it is mindful of its former fall" (lines 395–399).

Part 2: Vocabulary

Unlike some vocabulary tests, items like this require students to read and comprehend the text in order to determine the meaning of the word in context.

1. What does the word *vanity* mean in these lines from the text "Daedalus and Icarus"?

"Proud of his success, the foolish Icarus forsook his guide, and, bold in vanity, began to soar" (lines 348–350)

a. arrogance

b. fear

c. heroism

d. enthusiasm

2. Which word from the lines of text in Question 1 above best helps the reader understand the meaning of vanity?

a. proud

b. success

c. foolish

d. soar

Part 3: Prose Constructed Response

To write a successful response to the following prompt, students need to draw on material from two texts and develop their own approach to the question.

Use what you have learned from reading "Daedalus and Icarus" by Ovid and "To a Friend Whose Work Has Come to Triumph" by Anne Sexton to write an essay that provides an analysis of how Sexton transforms "Daedalus and Icarus." As a starting point, you may want to consider what is emphasized, absent, or different in the two texts, but feel free to develop your own focus for analysis. Develop your essay by providing textual evidence from both texts. Be sure to follow the conventions of standard English.

Teachers should note that PARCC has not broken down how much time should be spent on each part of the literary analysis task, only that a total of 80 minutes is allotted to complete it.

Figure 8.2 shows our recommendation on how to allot one's time using the formula in the previous section.

Depending on how much experience students have had reading poetry, our time allotment for reading the two poems may not be accurate. Teachers, who know their students best, can adjust accordingly.

Figure 8.2 Allocation of Time for Poetry Analysis

	Example with the PARCC (80 min.)
Read the two poems. Tenth graders should read at about 220 words per minute according to Carver, 1989. However, poetry takes longer to read and to comprehend, so we have doubled the length of time.	Total number of words in the two poems: 1108 divided by 220 = 5 minutes, multiplied by 2 = 10 minutes.
Answer two questions in Parts 1 and 2. Time how long it takes you to answer the questions and multiply by 3 to give your students enough time. We took 1.5 minutes to do these (1.5 × 3 = 4.5, rounded up to 5 minutes).	5 minutes
Subtract the amount of time for the multiple choice from the total time to find out how much time remains to write the essay.	80 – 15 = 65 min.
Multiply remaining time by .25 to calculate planning time.	65 min. × .25 = 16 min.
Multiply remaining time by .50 to calculate drafting time.	65 min × .50 = 32.5, rounded up to 33 min.
Multiply remaining time by .25 to calculate revising time.	65 min × .25 = 16 min.

PLC ACTIVITY: PROMPT ANALYSIS

Online 8.4
Prompt Analysis Questions

In Chapter 7, we explained how students can use the five PAQs (Prompt Analysis Questions) to understand what a writing prompt is asking them to do. It also can be useful to do prompt analysis with a group of colleagues. In your PLC, choose a prompt to analyze together. Use the Prompt Analysis Questions from Chapter 7 to guide your discussion. Keep in mind that prompts vary radically in the types and amount of information they provide to students about the kind of writing expected, so it may not be possible to answer every question for each prompt or assignment. However, learning to ask and answer a series of questions about the claim/topic, audience, purpose/mode, strategies, and role enables students to discern what is required of them and generate ideas for meeting that requirement.

In your PLC, you will probably discuss the meaning of terms like *claim*, distinguishing it from *topic*, acknowledging that an argument rests on a claim, although to some extent all writing can be described as an argument. At the same time, some prompts specify a particular topic (like the role of experience in learning) on which the claim needs to be based. Content area teachers may also need some explanation of the relationship between *purpose* and *mode*. The purpose designated by the prompt—to explain, to describe, to argue and so on—will usually dictate the mode of writing to be used. At the same time that teachers discuss the modes, it is a good idea to indicate that the modes frequently blur into one another because it's very difficult to write an explanation without some description or argue without explanation.

In analyzing the prompts for the CCSS assessments, the discussion may become quite spirited. Teachers have been very critical of the quality of these prompts, and doing a prompt analysis may bring this out. Acknowledge everyone's opinions, and keep in mind that writing on demand is only one genre of writing. It is not the be-all and end-all of what a writer should be able to do. If teachers find the prompts especially lacking, it may be productive to use the PAQ protocol to create some of your own prompts for use in various classrooms. We have turned around the questions so they can be used to *create* prompts, not just *analyze* them. The handout we use when guiding teachers through the process of creating their own prompts is shown in Figure 8.3.

If your PLC has time, we encourage you to have everyone actually write in response to the prompt you just analyzed or the one you just created. When we do this, we find that we develop empathy for students in a testing situation. We also usually find additional points of discussion, such as a realization that some prompts may be more challenging for some students. If you choose to analyze the tenth-grade PARCC prompt on Daedalus and Icarus, for example, you might realize how important an understanding of and comfort with reading poetry is. If your curriculum doesn't include much reading of poetry until eleventh and twelfth grade, then your tenth graders might find this prompt especially challenging.

As a final step in your PLC, discuss how to use these prompt analysis questions with students. The goal of doing so is to help students shift away from believing that prompts and assignments are designed to confound them; instead, they can see prompts and assignments as language with which they can engage and ultimately succeed.

Figure 8.3 Prompt Analysis Questions (PAQs) for Creating Rhetorically Based Writing Assignments

Online 8.5
Prompt Analysis Questions (PAQs) for Creating Rhetorically Based Writing Assignments

1. What is the *central claim/topic* called for?
What choices will students have to make with regard to this claim/topic? Will they need to focus the claim/topic in order to write a good essay? What arguments could students make for this claim? What do students know about this topic?

_____

_____

_____

_____

2. Who is the intended *audience*?
Will you name the audience specifically or leave it up to the student to infer? If you are creating an imagined audience, what will your students know about this particular audience? Do students know what kinds of expectations this audience has?

_____

_____

_____

_____

3. What is the *purpose/mode* for the writing task?
What is the purpose of this writing assignment? What is this writing supposed to accomplish? What mode of writing (narration, exposition, description, argument) or combination of modes are you expecting from your students? How will they be able to glean the expected mode from your prompt?

_____

_____

_____

_____

Figure 8.3 Prompt Analysis Questions (PAQs) for Creating Rhetorically Based Writing Assignments *(continued)*

4. What *strategies* will be most effective?

What does the purpose/mode suggest about possible strategies? Of the strategies your students are comfortable using—strategies like examples, definitions, analysis, classification, cause/effect, compare/contrast—which will be most effective here? Are there any strategies—such as number of examples or type of support—that you will specify as required?

_____

_____

_____

_____

5. What *role* should the writer assume to achieve the purpose?

Are you assigning a specific role like *applicant* or *representative*? If students are not assigned a specific role, what does the prompt or assignment tell them about the level of expertise they should demonstrate, the stance they should assume, or the approach(es) they should take?

_____

_____

_____

_____

Draft your prompt here:

_____

_____

_____

_____

_____

_____

_____

_____

_____

_____

Classroom Moves: How to Use Social Media to Develop On-Demand Writing Skills

People of a certain age often say "Thank goodness Facebook wasn't around when I was young," implying that we might have impulsively posted something then that we would now regret. There is a kind of immediacy when we text or tweet or write a status update on Facebook. Few of us go through the writing process or pause to mull over a draft before we make it available to our friends through social media. In that sense, much of the writing done today is a kind of writing on demand.

Students are already experts at writing on demand. As Daniels, Zemelman, and Steineke point out, "They are texting their friends on cell phones, writing and receiving instant messages, maintaining robust email correspondences, blogging, creating websites, updating their MySpace pages, publishing their poems or stories online, creating labyrinthine fantasy tales and games, composing songs and lyrics with software like GarageBand, making and sharing video clips, hanging out in chat rooms, or joining threaded discussions" (3).

Obviously, this kind of writing on demand is not the same as writing on demand for a test. However, it is worth building on the skills students already have when preparing them for the unique demands of the timed writing assessment.

For example, we know that students build fluency when they have many opportunities to do low-stakes, Level 1 writing. Let's look at some examples of how to capitalize on students' out-of-school writing skills.

Read and Text Something

This is a variation of a strategy from Project CRISS[1] called "read and say something" that encourages active reading. Students pair up to read a challenging text. At the end of each paragraph, page, section, or chapter—whatever block of

---

[1] Project CRISS is an educational initiative designed to help students of all abilities learn content information across the curriculum and throughout the grade levels. It offers professional development for teachers working to address the CCSS. http://www.projectcriss.com/

text makes sense for your reading passage and grade level—students stop and say something to each other about the chapter. This version has them text each other. Given this generation's facility with texting, pausing to text is probably less of an interruption than stopping to say something. This is great because it's important for the student to dive right back into the reading after a moment to process the text enough to say something about it to a classmate. What's to keep them from sending another text, and another and another, forgetting about the reading altogether? For accountability, monitor phone use and/or have students take a screen shot of their text trail to send you. What if some students don't have phones? Would it be possible to reserve some laptops or iPads for them to use?

Chat Room Research Forum

In this activity, students are given a short article on a controversial topic. They are then invited to a chat room explicitly designed to explore the topic. The challenge? For each thing they say about the topic, they have to make some reference to their article.

Facebook Status Updates

Online 8.6
*Facebook
Assignment*

This one works best with a lengthier text like a novel or a historical period. Kelly's methods students created this activity for a seventh-grade English class that was reading *Roll of Thunder, Hear My Cry*. Students chose a character from the novel, and as they read they wrote status updates from that character's point of view. This encourages students to get to know the characters better and imagine them as a part of their social network. Daily status updates build fluency, and if you want to change it into a larger assessment, the assignment and rubric can be found in our online resources.

Here are some sample status updates written by students about the character Jeremy in the novel:

> I feel really bad about that fire. I hadn't realized they lost almost all their land.
> April 7, 1933 4:52 P.M.

I better go check on them Logans up at the house.
April 4, 1933 4:04 A.M.

It was some hard work pumping that water.
April 4, 1933 4:01 A.M

Can't believe T.J. is being friends with R.W. and Melvin!!
February 1, 1933 6:48 P.M.

When I handed Mama the nuts, Cassie actually went nuts.
December 25, 1932 3:15 P.M.

Going to Mr. Barnett's store to go get some more nuts!
November 30, 1932 8:09 A.M.

Sitting by the fire, talking, and telling stories with my family!
November 14, 1932 10:34 P.M.

I'm ashamed to walk to school and see the Confederate flag over
the American flag.
November 2, 1932 7:37 A.M

Having a nice glass of milk after walking home with the Logans.
October 19, 1932 2:45 P.M

Why do my sisters have to be so mean to me?
October 13, 1932 9:03 A.M.

These students also create an "About Me" page for Jeremy online. Entries on Stacy
can be found here: https://sites.google.com/site/rothmyunit/home/rothmc/stacy.

The Major Shift Between Writing on Demand Pre–CCSS and Post–CCSS

In this chapter, our analysis of two Common Core Assessments—an eleventh-grade performance task from SBAC and a tenth-grade one from PARCC—revealed that reading is an integral part of both assessments. SBAC specifically allocates testing time to have students read the texts, take notes on them, and answer questions about them. PARCC does not break out the reading and writing time, which means students have to make a judgment themselves about how much time to spend reading and how much to spend writing.

In the past, teachers often worried about students freezing up as they faced a blank page, and that is still, of course, a concern. So it is worthwhile to help students feel comfortable with a variety of invention strategies like those in Chapter 4. But it's not enough. In the age of Common Core, teachers need to make sure that students understand the reading and don't get frozen or frustrated before they get to the writing. This need is complicated by the amount of reading students have to do before they even get to the text selection they are to draw from for their writing because of all the computer screens they have to go through.

For example, the eighth-grade ELA performance task requires students to read several articles about the production of pennies. But before students even get to the penny articles, they have to click through several screens, in which they verify their identity, select the test they wish to take, and learn about how to navigate the test. On the page with test instructions, as seen in the nearby figure, there are thirteen screens of instructions to scroll through. That's right: *thirteen*.

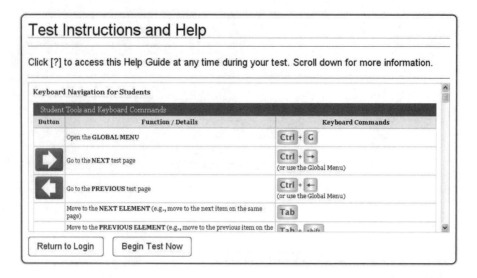

Once students actually get to the test questions, more scrolling is involved. They have to scroll through student directions—followed by four articles about the penny—in a skinny left-hand column, while reading the test questions in the right-hand column.

Before even getting to the first of the four articles of the penny, students have to read through about 300 words of directions. Once they get to the articles, they are expected to read articles within their text complexity band. All of this is going to be challenging for most students, but knowing how to manage their time can help them meet the challenge.

Notes on College Readiness

Teachers may feel that they and their students are putting a tremendous amount of time and effort into a very specific skill that may not matter once students pass the Common Core assessments. However, writing on demand is a necessary skill for college as well. College students are regularly asked to demonstrate their knowledge of subject matter in a variety of disciplines through essay exams. We know of students who have taken up to forty essay exams during their four-year program, and all college students have to produce writing under time pressures.

In conclusion, dealing with time—the dimension that distinguishes writing on demand from other genres of writing—is complex and can be taught explicitly to help students develop metacognitive skills about how they think of time in a testing situation. Time is just one element of the testing context, however. Analyzing the test context, including analyzing the prompt, can help prepare students for success on the new Common Core assessments. Part of this preparation should include attention to the kinds of reading involved, whether reading poetry or directions on multiple computer screens. Negotiating technology may be a factor in managing time. Therefore, building on the technology skills that students already have may be the best use of classroom time when preparing students to handle a timed writing situation.

Chapter Nine

Writing in Sentences

CHAPTER OVERVIEW *This chapter provides strategies for:*

- *analyzing the role of sentences in the Common Core State Standards*

- *helping students write better transitions*

- *showing students how to analyze their sentence structure and then vary it*

- *experimenting with passive and active voice to strengthen sentences*

- *revising sentences for stylistic effect*

- *explaining how syntax can be varied for effect.*

entences are the building blocks of writing. Each one carries its own weight, and together, when they are well formed, they create passages of effective prose. Strategies for writing clear, varied, and well-formed sentences are essential to teaching writing.

Sentence skills are important on the CCSS for another reason as well: Sentence-level knowledge is absolutely necessary for a variety of challenging multiple-choice and short-answer questions.

Sentences in the Common Core State Standards

What's new with sentences and the CCSS? Let's compare how skill with sentences is described in the National Council for Teachers of English standards versus the CCS standards (see Figure 9.1).

173

Figure 9.1 Comparing Standards: Skill with Sentences

NCTE Standard #6	CCSS Language Standard #3
Students apply knowledge of language structure, language conventions (e.g., spelling and punctuation), media techniques, figurative language, and genre to create, critique, and discuss print and nonprint texts.	Students apply knowledge of language to understand how language functions in different contexts, to make effective choices for meaning or style, and to comprehend more fully when reading or listening.

Published jointly by NCTE and the International Reading Association (IRA) in 1996, *The Standards for the English Language Arts* is designed to complement other national, state, and local standards and contributes to ongoing discussion about English language arts classroom activities and curricula. Visit http://www.ncte.org /standards.

Online 9.1
NCTE Standards

In both standards, knowledge of language, which includes sentence structure, is not presented as a separate unit of knowledge but, rather, as knowledge to be applied in reading, writing, and discussing. Furthermore, the Common Core standard includes references to context and choice. Students should develop a sense for what kinds of sentences work in specific contexts and how sentence structure choices affect their writing. For example, in the context of an email message, short sentences are most effective for busy readers plowing through loads of messages in their in-boxes. In contrast, a report that includes complicated scientific data will require some longer, more complex sentences. Another difference—create, critique, and discuss—speaks to issues of revising and comprehending. A complete list of NCTE standards can be found in our online materials.

Online 9.2
Grade-Level Breakdown of CCSS Writing Standard #1: Sentences

The CCSS do not have a separate standard on sentences, which is appropriate since sentences are part of larger wholes. Language about sentences does appear in the first three writing standards, and these are worth examining. To make it easier to see what these standards say about sentences, see Figure 9.2 where we have italicized the language that is different from grade to grade within the same standard.

Figure 9.2 Grade-Level Breakdown of CCSS Writing Standard #1: Sentences

Anchor Writing Standard #1 for grades 6–8: Write arguments to support claims with clear reasons and relevant evidence.			Anchor Writing Standard #1 for grades 9–12: Write arguments to support claims *in an analysis of substantive topics or texts, using valid reasoning and relevant and sufficient* evidence.	
Grade 6	**Grade 7**	**Grade 8**	**Grades 9/10**	**Grades 11/12**
1c. Use words, phrases, and clauses to *clarify* the relationships among claim(s) and reasons.	1c. Use words, phrases, and clauses to *create cohesion and clarify* the relationships among claim(s), reasons, and evidence.	1c. Use words, phrases, and clauses to create cohesion and clarify the relationships among claim(s), *counterclaims*, reasons, and evidence.	1c. Use words, phrases, and clauses to *link the major sections of the text*, create cohesion, and clarify the relationships *between claim(s) and reasons, between reasons and evidence, and between claim(s) and counterclaims.*	1c. Use words, phrases, and clauses *as well as varied syntax* to link the major sections of the text, create cohesion, and clarify the relationships between claim(s) and reasons, between reasons and evidence, and between claim(s) and counterclaims. 2c. Use appropriate and varied transitions and syntax to link the major sections of the text, create cohesion, and clarify the relationships among complex ideas and concepts.

(continues)

Figure 9.2 Grade-Level Breakdown of CCSS Writing Standard #1: Sentences *(continued)*

Grade 6	Grade 7	Grade 8	Grades 9/10	Grades 11/12
				3d. Use precise words and phrases, telling details, and sensory language to convey a vivid picture of the experiences, events, setting, and/or characters.

Online 9.3
CCSS Writing Standard #2 and Sentences

As we can see, in Language Standard #1, writers are expected to use "phrases and clauses" to strengthen the argument by linking together claims, counterclaims, reasons, and evidence. Sentence skills are not evaluated separately; they serve the larger argument. In Writing Standard #2 (see Figure 9.3) about the informative/explanatory mode, sentences

Figure 9.3 CCSS Writing Standard #2 and Sentences

Anchor Writing Standard #2: Write informative/explanatory texts to examine and convey complex ideas and information clearly and accurately through the effective selection, organization, and analysis of content.				
Grade 6	**Grade 7**	**Grade 8**	**Grades 9/10**	**Grades 11/12**
2c. Use appropriate transitions to clarify the relationships among ideas and concepts.	2c. Use appropriate transitions to *create cohesion* and clarify the relationships among ideas and concepts.	2c. Use appropriate *and varied* transitions to create cohesion and clarify the relationships among ideas and concepts.	2c. Use appropriate and varied transitions to *link the major sections of the text*, create cohesion, and clarify the relationships among *complex* ideas and concepts.	2c. Use appropriate and varied transitions *and syntax* to link the major sections of the text, create cohesion, and clarify the relationships among complex ideas and concepts.

are not mentioned at all, nor are phrases and clauses. However, there is mention of a particular kind of sentence—the transition sentence—and its ability to improve the clarity and cohesion of the writing.

Like Standard #2, Standard #3 makes only indirect references to sentences as it describes the qualities expected in effective narratives, as one can see in Figure 9.4.

Were you able to spot the sentence standards? Yes, we had to squint too. Sentences are not mentioned in the anchor part of the standard (the part in the top row). Instead, we find them in the detailed descriptions at each grade level, and, even then, the word "sentence" is not specifically used; instead, the standards specify the use of "phrases and clauses" for specific purposes. A sentence is an independent clause. Sentences can contain phrases and clauses. According to these standards, writers are to manipulate the structure of sentences for specific purposes. For example, sentences are used mainly to create cohesion and unity in a piece of writing and to contribute to organization through the use of transition phrases.

Online 9.4
*CCSS Writing
Standard #3 and
Sentences*

Figure 9.4 CCSS Writing Standard #3 and Sentences

Anchor Writing Standard #3 for grades 6–8: Write narratives to develop real or imagined experiences or events using effective technique, relevant descriptive details, and well-structured event sequences.			Anchor Writing Standard #3 for grades 9–12: Write narratives to develop real or imagined experiences or events using effective technique, *well-chosen* details, and well-structured event sequences.	
Grade 6	**Grade 7**	**Grade 8**	**Grades 9/10**	**Grades 11/12**
3c. Use a variety of transition words, phrases, and clauses to convey sequence and signal shifts from one time frame or setting to another.	3c. Use a variety of transition words, phrases, and clauses to convey sequence and signal shifts from one time frame or setting to another.	3c. Use a variety of transition words, phrases, and clauses to convey sequence and signal shifts from one time frame or setting to another, *and show the relationships among experiences and events.*	3c. Use a variety of techniques to sequence events *so that they build on one another to create a coherent whole.*	3c. Use a variety of techniques to sequence events so that they build on one another to create a coherent whole *and build toward a particular tone and outcome (e.g., a sense of mystery, suspense, growth, or resolution).*

Online 9.5
Strategies for Cohesive Ties

Figure 9.5 Strategies for Cohesive Ties

Strategy	Example
Repeat key words	The band director emphasized precision. When he introduced a new formation, he gave section leaders precise directions about location.
Repeat sentence patterns	Because my brother was good at science, everyone in my family expected me to be at home in the lab. Because my sister was a great musician, they thought I should join the band.
Use synonyms	In the Internet world, some people take on alternate identities. These disguises can help them cheat others.

Essays that use the greatest number of cohesive ties—words and phrases that create transitions between sentences—typically receive higher scores on timed writing tests than those that use only a few. Figure 9.5 shows some strategies students can use to accomplish this.

There are many words that signal relationships between sentences, and helping students become familiar with them is another way to develop cohesion in their writing. It is not enough to just provide students with a list of these words and phrases, however; students should also be guided to think about *when* they might be most useful. Figure 9.6 shows some of these occasions.

Online 9.6
Occasions for Using Transitional Words

Figure 9.6 Occasions for Using Transitional Words

Occasions for Creating Cohesion	Transitional Words and Phrases
Narrations or descriptions or processes that include time	after, during, next, again, every time, the next day, always, finally, then, before, meanwhile, while
Descriptions that convey relationships among things/people	around here, on the side of, behind, in front of, on top of, below, in the center, over
Explanations of the relative importance of things or ideas	first, less important, more important, mainly, second

Figure 9.6 Occasions for Using Transitional Words *(continued)*

Occasions for Creating Cohesion	Transitional Words and Phrases
Comparing and contrasting	also, than, similarly, as, likewise, either/or, neither/nor, in the same way, also, yet, however, but, on the contrary, instead, unlike
Describing cause-and-effect relationships	although, as a result, since, because, if/then, so that, consequently, for this reason, therefore
Introducing examples	as, like, for example, such as, namely, to illustrate
Signaling emphasis	indeed, in fact, in other words
Offering more information	in addition, besides, moreover, also, similarly, furthermore

Sentences in the Language Standard

In addition to writing standards, we find sentences mentioned in Language Standard #3. Figure 9.7 looks at the progression of the language standards related to sentences in grades 6–12.

Online 9.7
Progression of Language Standard #3

This language standard poses challenges to teachers because each grade level seemingly points to new and different skills, unlike other Common Core standards that seem to build on a particular skill from grade to grade. Therefore, we will provide sentence activities for each skill: varying sentence structure (grade 6), writing concisely (grade 7), using active and passive voice and mood in verbs (grade 8), editing sentences for style (grades 9/10), and varying syntax for effect (grades 11/12).

Varying Sentence Structure (Grade 6)

One of the characteristics of good writing, one that gets high marks from evaluators of writing tests, is variety in sentence structure. The CCSS suggest focusing on this skill in

Figure 9.7 Progression of Language Standard #3

Language Standard #3: Use knowledge of language and its conventions when writing, speaking, reading, or listening.		*Apply* knowledge of language to *understand how language functions in different contexts, to make effective choices for meaning or style, and to comprehend more fully when reading or listening.*		
Grade 6	**Grade 7**	**Grade 8**	**Grades 9/10**	**Grades 11/12**
3a. Vary sentence patterns for meaning, reader/listener interest, and style. 3b. Maintain consistency in style and tone.	3a. *Choose language that expresses ideas precisely and concisely, recognizing and eliminating wordiness and redundancy.*	3a. *Use verbs in the active and passive voice and in the conditional and subjunctive mood to achieve particular effects (e.g., emphasizing the actor or the action; expressing uncertainty or describing a state contrary to fact).*	3a. *Write and edit work so that it conforms to the guidelines in a style manual (e.g., MLA Handbook, Turabian's Manual for Writers) appropriate for the discipline and writing type.*	3a. *Vary syntax for effect, consulting references (e.g., Tufte's Artful Sentences) for guidance as needed; apply an understanding of syntax to the study of complex texts when reading.*

the sixth grade. Of course, syntactic variety is partly shaped by word choice. Using strong verbs often leads writers to move away from repeating the following pattern:

NOUN [SUBJECT] VERB ADJECTIVE [COMPLEMENT]

The sports field was rectangular.

At the same time, however, making good syntactic choices requires thinking about the audience. Writers need to consider where they want to direct the audience's attention and then create the syntax to accomplish their goals. Consider, for example, the following sentences.

Lacrosse is my sister's sport. It is strenuous and challenging.

The linear form shown above, which puts one subject-verb-complement sentence after another, is typical for many inexperienced writers, but this form makes it difficult for the writer to direct the audience's attention to the connection between the features of lacrosse and the game itself. Here is an alternative:

> *Lacrosse, strenuous and challenging, is my sister's sport.*

Putting the adjectives *strenuous* and *challenging* in the same sentence instead of adding that information in a separate sentence focuses the reader's attention on the nature of lacrosse, making it easier to move on to another sentence like this:

> *It attracts some of the strongest athletes in our school.*

The previous two sentences direct the audience to qualities of the sport. If the writer wants to focus the audience in a slightly different way, an alternative like this can be used:

> *Attracting some of the strongest athletes in our school, lacrosse is my sister's strenuous and challenging sport.*

Here the audience is directed to think more about the implications of lacrosse for a school's athletic program. In other words, syntactic choices are linked to quality in writing because they play such a key role in demonstrating the writer's purposes and directing the audience's attention.

Online 9.8
Identifying
Sentence Types

To help students develop an awareness of sentence structure, teachers can show them how to analyze the kind of sentence structure they are currently using. This is best done within the context of a writing assignment students are already invested in, rather than as a separate, decontextualized exercise. For example, this sixth-grade student was writing a guide to living in family housing on a university campus. Her purpose was to orient other children like herself to living in this particular environment. She had been through several drafts and had gotten some feedback on her work. The information in Figure 9.8 can be used to help a student analyze her or his sentence patterns.

Figure 9.8 Identifying Sentence Types

Sentence Type	Features	Example	Symbol
Simple	One independent clause (can have compound subject and/or compound predicate)	Traders and buyers hurry to the center of town and usually arrive at the same time.	S

(continues)

Figure 9.8 Identifying Sentence Types *(continued)*

Sentence Type	Features	Example	Symbol
Compound	Two or more independent clauses but no dependent clause. Independent clauses may be joined by a comma and coordinating conjunction *or* by a semicolon with or without conjunctive adverb.	The guide dog stopped suddenly, so he did not fall into the hole. Rain poured for ten days; therefore, the festival had to be cancelled.	CD
Complex	One independent clause and one or more dependent clauses	She read the newspaper because she wanted to learn more about the candidates for mayor.	CX
Compound-complex	Two or more coordinated independent clauses and at least one dependent clause	He majored in biology, but he became so fascinated by language that he changed to English.	CD-CX

Here is Sun Min's draft:

Making Friends

    If you just moved, you might wonder about how to make friends or you might even worry about having no friends (CX). Well, don't worry any more—we have a solution (CD)!

    Plan a barbecue (BBQ) with your neighbors (S). This will give you a chance to talk with each other and get to know each other (S). For example, we had a BBQ to welcome our new neighbors from Germany (S). Our mom made a special dish—Korean ribs (S). Our Italian neighbors brought a pasta salad (S).

If you want to make friends, don't be shy (CX). Play with other kids (S). They will be your friends if you treat them nicely (CD). For example, my brother met a friend when he was playing basketball (S). His ball got stuck behind the backboard, and another kid came along and helped him get it down (CD). Soon Daniel and this kid were playing together (S). I became friends with Annette when Annette was new to the neighborhood (CX). I helped Annette feel comfortable when she first arrived, and soon we were great friends (CD-CX).

Maybe you can find a way to make other people in the neighborhood feel comfortable too (S).

The sentence analysis of the draft above revealed the following numbers of types of sentences:

Simple sentences: 9

Compound sentences: 3

Complex sentences: 3

Compound-Complex sentences: 1

This sentence-type analysis revealed that she relied heavily on one type—the simple sentence. The implication is clear for this writer: Although there are a number of good qualities in this piece, the writer can improve it by using a greater variety of sentence types. For example, the following two simple sentences at the end of the second paragraph can easily be combined with a coordinating conjunction, and doing so makes sense because both simple sentences are about the kind of food served at the BBQ:

Before: Our mom made a special dish—Korean ribs (S). Our Italian neighbors brought a pasta salad (S).

After sentence combining: Our mom made a special dish—Korean ribs, and our Italian neighbors brought a pasta salad (CD).

Similarly, the first two sentences of the third paragraph can be combined because their meaning is so similar:

If you want to make friends, don't be shy; play with other kids (CD-CX).

Using sentence analysis to help students vary their sentence structure helps them improve their sentence sense and leads to more robust revision. Students may begin to think about the content of their writing as well. For example, with some prompting,

Sun Min could see that her text was really about more than one solution, as her topic sentence stated. Also, the final simple sentence perhaps could do a bit more work than it was currently doing.

A Flesch-Kincaid analysis of Sun Min's writing showed it was at the 4.8 grade level, but after making changes like those above, the revised passage that follows was at the 5.7 grade level:

Making Friends

If you just moved to family housing, you might wonder about how to make friends or you might even worry about having no friends. Well, don't worry any more—I have some solutions!

To start, plan a barbecue (BBQ) with your neighbors. This will give you a chance to talk with each other and get to know each other. For example, we had a BBQ to welcome our new neighbors from Germany. Our mom made a special dish—Korean ribs, and our Italian neighbors brought a pasta salad.

If you want to make friends, don't be shy; play with other kids. They will be your friends if you treat them nicely. For example, my brother met a friend when he was playing basketball. His ball got stuck behind the backboard, and another kid came along and helped him get it down. Soon Daniel and this kid were playing together. Another example is about how I became friends with Annette when Annette was new to the neighborhood. I helped Annette feel comfortable when she first arrived, and soon we were great friends.

After you have lived here for a while, maybe you can find a way to make other people in the neighborhood feel comfortable too.

The fact is that most writers prefer one sentence type—even unconsciously—and simply becoming aware of that preference can help them introduce more variety into their writing. In addition, many writers favor particular forms of a given type of sentence. For example, one person may like to begin many complex sentences with the dependent clause (*Although it was a cold day, the children went swimming.*) rather than putting it at the end of the sentence. Another person may love the coordinating conjunction *and*, using it continually to connect two independent clauses in a compound sentence. Once students have identified the types of sentences they most commonly use, the next step is to look for recurring patterns within those types.

Students will use sentence variety effectively when they consider the effects they want to achieve. The following steps, then, can lead to successful use of sentence variety:

- Learn to identify the four major sentence types—simple, compound, complex and compound-complex.
- Consider how the syntax of these types will direct the reader's attention.
- Identify sentence types in one's own writing.
- Analyze the patterns of sentence types in one's own writing.
- Consider what arrangement of sentence types will achieve the desired effect.

Our interviews with successful on-demand writers revealed that they had this kind of sentence knowledge. Here are a couple of examples:

> I have an individual style. Some sentences will be short and then I'll have one that's three or four lines long. I try to break things up this way, and I try to make it dramatic by making a sentence of just a few words.
>
> *—Maya*

> When I'm trying to be descriptive, I'll use a longer sentence, and when I'm trying to make a point, I use shorter sentences.
>
> *—Swathi*

Writing Concisely (Grade 7)

The Common Core Language Standard for grade 7 has a different focus: "Choose language that expresses ideas precisely and concisely, recognizing and eliminating wordiness and redundancy." Here is an example of writing by a seventh grader who wrote a practice essay in response to the Amelia Earhart prompt. Her second paragraph was wordy and redundant:

> She had to do a lot of planning with a lot of people to have these flights take place. She made some of these plans with George Putnam. They made plans for Amelia to be the first woman and second person to fly alone across the Atlantic. She became fond of him as their friendship grew; they were married before the crossing. (62 words)

To make this part of her essay more concise, this student could combine the first three sentences in the previous paragraph to make these two sentences:

> One of Amelia Earhart's challenges was planning. With the help of George Putnam, she planned to be the first woman and the second person to fly alone across the Atlantic. Amelia grew fond of George as they did this planning—their friendship grew, and before the flight took place, they were married. (52 words)

Sentence combining requires writers to weave several short sentences into a single longer one that adheres to conventions of standard written English. In the previous example, not only is the word length reduced by 16 percent, but the meaning is more precise in this revision. However, this skill needs to be modeled and nurtured by giving many opportunities to practice. The skill is measured by the number of combinations one can create.

RESEARCH AND POLITICAL CONSIDERATIONS

Sentence combining grew out of the transformational grammar movement in the 1960s (initiated by Noam Chomsky), and transformational sentence combining as a way of teaching writing was first taught in 1963, according to a 1970 article in *The English Journal* (Stryker). Mellon's 1969 study of seventh graders showed improvement in "syntactic maturity" in the writing of students who had done sentence-combining activities. Several other studies found much the same result. More recent research also supports the efficacy of sentence combining. It was one of eleven strategies shown to improve student writing through a meta-analysis of research studies in the report *Writing Next*. Here is how sentence combining was defined in the report:

> Sentence combining is an alternative approach to more traditional grammar instruction. Sentence-combining instruction involves teaching students to construct more complex and sophisticated sentences through exercises in which two or more basic sentences are combined into a single sentence.
> In one approach, students at higher and lower writing levels are paired to receive six lessons that teach (a) combining smaller related sentences into a compound sentence using the connectors *and*, *but*, and *because*; (b) embedding an adjective or adverb from one sentence into another; (c) creating complex sentences by embedding an adverbial and adjectical clause from

one sentence into another; and (d) making multiple embeddings involving adjectives, adverbs, adverbial clauses, and adjectival clauses. The instructor provides support and modeling and the student pairs work collaboratively to apply the skills taught. (Graham and Perin 2007, 18)

Classroom Moves

To help students develop sentence combining skills, start with this series of short sentences:

1. An atom is too small to see.
2. Atoms are made of electrons, protons, and neutrons.
3. The center of every atom is the nucleus.
4. The nucleus makes up 99.9 percent of the mass of every atom.
5. The nucleus makes up only one trillionth of the volume of an atom.

These sentences can be combined into one: Although an atom is too small to see, we know they are made of electrons, protons, and neutrons and that every atom has a nucleus at its center, which makes up 99.9 percent of the mass of an atom, yet only one trillionth of the volume.

After modeling the previous sentence, give students this new set of sentences. See how many different ways they can combine the following sentences into one:

1. Last week I took the train into the city.
2. My sister went with me.
3. We spent the day in the public library.
4. We were looking for information on our family's genealogy.
5. We found records dating back to 1642.

Have students share with a partner.

Next, give students a longer set of sentences:

Set One

1. The wedding was over.

2. The guests were tired.

3. The guests were happy.

4. The bride and groom were ready to leave.

5. The guests got into their cars.

6. Their cars filled the parking lot.

7. They laughed and talked.

8. Suddenly the parking lot was empty.

This time—after students have combined these sentences—have them share in small groups, comparing their versions with those written by other students. Discuss which they prefer and why. Are there some sentences that would be more effective in some situations rather than in others? This will help students understand that sentence composition involves making choices and that those choices have different effects on the reader.

Again, have students combine the following sentences, this time sharing their versions aloud or on the board.

Set Two

1. My desk is cluttered.

2. It is covered with papers.

3. It is covered with books.

4. My assignment is somewhere on the desk.

5. I can't find my assignment.

6. My teacher will be angry if I turn my assignment in late.

7. My teacher will lower my grade on the assignment.

8. I wish I could find my assignment.

Online 9.9
*Sentence
Combining
Exercises*

To connect these exercises with their own writing, have students look at some of their own writing in their journal or a current paper draft. Are there some creative ways in which they could combine sentences to make the writing more concise? If this part of the activity can be done on computer, students can use the "word count" feature of Microsoft Word (or another word processing program) to monitor whether they are indeed making their writing more concise. These sample sentence sets are available in our online materials.

Using Active and Passive Voice and Mood in Verbs (Grade 8)

In eighth grade, Language Standard #3 requires students to be able to "Use verbs in the active and passive voice and in the conditional and subjunctive mood to achieve particular effects (e.g., emphasizing the actor or the action; expressing uncertainty or describing a state contrary to fact)." We'll discuss active and passive voice first, followed by verb moods.

Writing strong sentences is very much about choice. Word choice is probably the most obvious aspect of sentences because we combine individual words to create sentences, and it's easy to see how word choice shapes sentences, which, in turn, contributes to the overall quality of writing. Selecting an apt word to express an idea will always be impressive to a reader, and strong verbs are particularly helpful. Consider, for example, the differences among these sentences:

> The ball was thrown by the coach.
> The coach threw the ball.
> The coach hurled the ball.

The move from passive voice (*was thrown*) to active voice (*coach threw*) makes the sentence more interesting, but the more precise verb *hurled* gives a much clearer picture of the action. Using an active verb like *hurled* makes the sentence more vivid and compelling. In general, word choice contributes to qualities that readers associate with good writing because appropriate language gives writing an authoritative quality. This is not to say that using big words is the same as using the right word. For example, we wouldn't use *hurled* instead of *threw* unless it is right for the context. Readers trust and respond positively to writers who use words well.

Choice depends on the context of the writing. For example, for scientific writing, passive voice is appropriate because what is being done—in an experiment, for example—is more important than who is doing it. However, for most other kinds of writing, active voice is a better choice.

Another way students can improve their sentence quality is by revising sentences to use more strong verbs. This means that verbs of being (*am*, *be*, *are*, *is*, *was*, and *were*) along with *had* and *has* should be eliminated where possible. For example, see how the weak verb in the following sentence has been replaced with one that creates a vivid image.

BEFORE: She has hair that is long and stringy.

AFTER: Her hair hangs below her waist in thread-like tendrils.

This activity will especially help students who are writing narratives, as expected in Writing Standard #3.

After students have completed this exercise, ask them to revise some of their own sentences. One way to facilitate this process is to collect some sentences with weak verbs from student papers and ask students to revise them; students nearly always recognize their own sentences in lists like these. Then they can swap drafts and underline weak sentences for one another to revise. Finally, they can identify and revise weak sentences in their own drafts.

Making choices about the conditional and subjunctive mood is more complex, in part because these are used in particular situations. We've noticed that students rarely use the subjunctive, perhaps because it sounds grammatically incorrect. Here is an example of the subjunctive mood, combined with the conditional:

If I *were* a millionaire, I would buy a Ferrari.
(subjunctive)   (conditional)

Students often want to use *was* instead of *were* in the sentence above because *was* seems to match the subject *I*. That would be correct if the sentence read like this:

When I was a millionaire, I bought a Ferrari.

The difference is that the example immediately above refers to something that actually happened, whereas the previous sentence deals with a condition—being a millionaire— that would have to happen before the Ferrari would be bought. (Note our use of passive voice here!) The clue to the need for the conditional mood is the word *if*. Another clue is the use of *would*, *could*, or *might*.

For students who are unused to using the subjunctive and conditional mood, have them use sentence frames to get started with constructing this kind of sentence:

If I were _____, I would _____.
If I were _____, I could _____.
If I were _____, I might _____.

Students can look for examples of subjunctive in their reading or the media and then imitate the form. For example, here is an advertising jingle:

> I <u>wish</u> I *were* an Oscar Mayer wiener.
> That is what I'd really like to be.
> 'Cause <u>if</u> I *were* an Oscar Mayer wiener,
> everyone would be in love with me.

Here is a sentence frame made from that jingle:

> I <u>wish</u> I *were* a(n) _____.
> That is what I'd really like to be.
> 'Cause <u>if</u> I *were* a(n) _____,
> everyone would be in love with me.

Many more examples of the subjunctive in the media can be found on this website: http://www.ceafinney.com/subjunctive/examples.html.

Moving from sentence frames to students' own writing can be tricky. The use of these moods is fairly rare, so it is hard to be sure students will have opportunities to apply the knowledge in authentic writing situations. An intermediate step is to have students do some quick-writes in their journals that deal with situations that are not factual. Here are some prompts:

- If you were fifteen feet tall, describe what it would be like for you to get to school.

- If you could be any animal you wish, what would you choose to be? Describe the new things you would learn about the world from the perspective of this animal.

- What if the United States were conquered by China? How would life change?

- What if you woke up one morning and found that one of your parents (or guardian) had changed into a giant spider. What would happen?

Editing Sentences for Style (Grades 9/10) and Varying Syntax for Effect (Grades 11/12)

In high school, the Common Core Language Standard (#3) emphasizes style and syntax of sentences. Models are essential for developing this kind of sentence sense. Students need to see the various effects achieved by other writers. Reading is, of course, an excellent way for students to see varieties of styles and use of syntax, but even students who read a great deal may need explicit instruction in identifying and using these strategies.

Imitation

Imitation offers a way to give students the ability to make choices about sentences. As we use it here, imitation does not mean simply copying the work of others; it means using models to generate creative ideas about syntax. One of the most common maxims is that good writers read widely. While it's true that extensive reading contributes to the quality of writing, the connection between the two can be strengthened if students are encouraged to see the texts they read as treasure troves to be mined for examples of effective, even arresting, sentences. The four steps of imitation are recognition, copying, understanding, and creative imitation.

Recognition

Online 9.10
Sentence Patterns I

The first step in the pedagogy of imitation is *recognition*, seeing sentence patterns. Teachers can always give students models for imitation exercises, but it is much more effective if students become collectors of sentences themselves. One way to help them get started with the process of recognition is to suggest patterns they might seek out. For example, students could begin with a list like the one shown in Figure 9.9. While the technical terms may be unfamiliar—even off-putting—to students, the content is important. The rhetorical labels and definitions can help students see that there are recognizable patterns with a long history of use and, further, that they can learn those patterns for writing effective sentences.

Copying

Once students become adept at recognizing sentences worth imitating, they can move to the next step in the imitation process: *copying*. This means actually transcribing the sentence, word for word, with all its punctuation. Some teachers find it useful to have students keep journals into which they copy sentences that impress them. The sentences could also be shared on one wall of the classroom. The location doesn't matter, but the process of copying does. The connections among the hand, eye, and brain, which are all engaged in copying, foster learning, and students can actually begin to learn new sentence patterns through the act of copying

Figure 9.9 Sentence Patterns I

Type	Features	Example
Multiple repetitions (Anaphora)	Repetition of same word(s) at the beginning of successive clauses.	Our class has worked on school spirit for four years—four years of pep rallies and bonfires, four years of cookie sales and tag days, four years of cheering ourselves hoarse.
Phrase reversal (Chiasmus)	The second half of a sentence reverses the order of the first.	When the going gets tough, the tough get going.
Interrupted repetition (Diacope)	Repetition of word or phrase with one or more words in between.	Give me bread, oh my jailer, give me bread.
End repetition (Epiphora)	Repetition of word or phrase at the end of several clauses.	When I was a child, I spoke as a child, I understood as a child, I thought as a child.
Apparent omission (Occupatio)	Emphasizing a point by seeming to pass over it.	I will not mention her extravagance, her luxurious wardrobe, her credit card debts, her loyalty to fashion designers—austerity is her new mode.
Part/whole substitution (Synecdoche)	Substitution of part for the whole.	All hands on deck.
Triple-Parallels (Tricolon)	Pattern of three parallel phrases.	I came, I saw, I conquered.
Verb repetition (Zeugma)	One verb governs several objects, each in a different way.	Here thou great Anna, whom three realms obey, dost sometimes counsel take—and sometimes tea.

Online 9.11
*Sentence
Patterns II*

Figure 9.10 Sentence Patterns II

Type	Features	Example
Reversal	State idea negatively and then positively.	The trouble is not with the facts; the trouble is that clear inferences have not been drawn from the facts.
Command	Use imperative voice at the beginning of a sentence to attract attention.	Never mind that the teacher gave him a pass, he was still suspended for skipping class.
Repeating	Repeat words for emphasis.	I scream for ice cream, you scream for ice cream, we all scream for ice cream.

Understanding

Understanding is the next step in the process of imitation. Once students have found (or been given) and copied effective sentences, they can analyze the sentences to figure out how they are constructed. Figure 9.10 provides a model they can use to analyze their sentences. By giving each sentence a name, describing its features, and including the sentence itself as an example, students develop a broader understanding of how sentences can be constructed.

Creative Imitation

Creative imitation is the final step in the process. At this point students are ready to generate sentences of their own, using the sentences of others as models. Like the experience of copying, this part of the process helps them develop new sentence sense because they are physically, visually, and mentally involved in creating new syntax. Here are some examples of creative imitations of sentences from Mark Twain's *Huckleberry Finn*:

> It was a mighty nice family and a mighty nice house too.

> *It was a mighty nice burger and a mighty nice rest'raunt too.*

> It was beautiful to hear that clock tick and sometimes when one of these peddlers had been along and scoured her up and got her in good shape, she would start in and strike a hundred and fifty before she got tuckered out.

> *It was grand to see that clown smile, and sometimes when one of these girls*
> *had been waiting on a young'un standing in front of that counter, she would*
> *hand him a placemat with the clown grinning from one side to the other.*

Imitation's progression from recognition of sentence patterns, to copying various patterns, to understanding patterns by analyzing them, to creatively imitating them helps students learn to produce as well as appreciate new sentence types.

Sentence Combining

Many students routinely employ the simple sentence and the compound sentence, using *and* as a coordinating conjunction, and they use this pattern again and again and again. To introduce a greater variety of sentence structures into their writing, students need to learn new patterns, and sentence combining can help because it enables students to learn to write more complex sentences. With the ability to write more complex sentences comes the capacity to introduce greater sentence variety in any piece of writing, including writing on demand.

Cued Sentence Combining

Sentence combining exercises can help students broaden their sentence sense. The first type is cued sentence combining, as shown below, where students are cued by indicating the word they should use in combining the two sentences.

Combine each pair of sentences into one sentence, using the word in parentheses, as shown in the example that follows.

1. Willa Cather wrote about life in the American west. She was raised in Nebraska. (use *who*)
   Willa Cather, who was raised in Nebraska, wrote about life in the American West.

2. My family moved to California. My father became a disk jockey. (use *when*)

3. All the sophomore girls traveled to Detroit. In Detroit they had a concert. (use *where*)

4. The burglar opened the closet door carefully. He was looking for a locked box. (use *and*)

5. Bald eagles are a protected species. The population of bald eagles is growing annually. (use *but*)

6. Soccer is often played in the spring. It is also played in the fall. (use *or*)

7. The price of the new CD has been increased. It is possible to purchase it with a money-saving coupon. (use *but*)

8. The boy carried water bottles for the football team. He was called Water Boy. (use *who*)

9. Oklahoma was the destination of the Cherokee people who were forced to move out of the Southeast in the early nineteenth century. It was called Indian Territory before it became a state. (use *which*)

Online 9.12
*Cued Sentence
Combining*

10. Commercial airplanes consume a lot of fuel. Some newer planes have been made more fuel efficient. (use *although*)

Open Sentence Combining

A less structured form of sentence combining, called open sentence combining, gives students a series of short sentences and asks them to combine them however they like. Usually students come up with several variations of combinations, and they can learn more about sentence variety by looking at one another's combinations in pairs or in small groups. They come to understand that there is no one right way to put sentences together, that different writers want to achieve different effects.

Cumulative Sentences

Sentence combining offers one way to help students develop the ability to vary their syntactic patterns, but other strategies are also available. One of these is to teach students the cumulative sentence. This pattern begins with an independent clause that is amplified by a series of free modifiers. Here are some examples:

The flame edged up the match

to

The flame edged up the match, driving a film of moisture and a thin strip of darker grey before it.

The skaters are filling the rink

to

The skaters are filling the rink, the girls gliding and spinning, the boys swooping and daring, their arms flapping like wings.

The baby cried

to

Lusty-voiced, red faced, with flailing legs and arms, the baby cried, wild as a hornet, tiny as a cat.

The NASCAR phenomenon has swept the country

to

The NASCAR phenomenon has swept the country, involving great numbers of car enthusiasts, drawing ever larger audiences, attracting big money from advertisers, enveloping even Barbie in its uniform.

The modifiers that follow the main clause add considerable detail, and they ask the writer to observe closely and choose words carefully. As Francis Christensen, an early proponent of the cumulative sentence, put it, writing cumulative sentences requires "verbal virtuosity and syntactical ingenuity" (1963, 160). Exercises like the one that follows can help students develop cumulative sentences.

Cumulative Sentence Exercise

Add at least three free modifiers to these main clauses, varying the position of the modifiers. Try to include as much sensory detail as possible.

Online 9.13
*Cumulative
Sentence Exercise*

1. Four women in red walked to the podium

2. Then I heard the siren blare

3. She raised her hand

4. The feather bed beckoned me

5. Five sparrows huddled near the bird bath

6. The speaker paused

7. Joan could play the piano for hours

8. The old man's eye remained fixed on me

9. Ocean swells moved rhythmically toward us

10. The little girl stood at the top of the stairs

Compare your cumulative sentences with someone else's, considering the kinds of details each of you adds to the main clause.

To sum up, in grades 9–12 the Common Core State Standards focus on editing sentences for style and varying syntax for effect. This section has provided a number of activities: use of models, imitation, cued sentence combining, open sentence combining, and the cumulative sentence activity to help students develop sentence sense. However, whenever these kinds of activities can be integrated into reading content material or writing authentically, the activities will be much more effective. To think about how to do this kind of integration, we suggest the following PLC activity.

PLC ACTIVITY: CREATING SENTENCE ACTIVITIES FOR DIFFERENT CONTENT AREA CLASSES

This PLC activity helps teachers find material in their content area that will help develop the kind of sentence sense that students need to improve as writers and to do well on the CCSS assessments. Members of the PLC should read through the sample assessment questions that deal with sentence work on their own and then create an activity that addresses the skill called for in the question. This activity should be from teacher's own subject area. When sharing the activity with the group and discussing it, use the following questions to help each other revise the activities for greater effectiveness.

1. How does this activity help students learn content material?

2. What kind of sentence skill does this help students develop?

3. How can this activity be differentiated for different learners?

Example: We chose the following assessment question from the SBAC eighth-grade ELA test:

> A student is writing an argumentative essay about physical education (PE) classes in middle school for her English assignment. The teachers suggested the student add an opening sentence that establishes a clear claim. Read the student's draft and the directions that follow.
>
> > Too many kids waste dozens of hours each week in front of the TV or computer. They may be exercising their fingers and sometimes their minds, but they are not exercising the rest of their bodies. But,

in physical education class, they do. Recent research has shown that physical education class has many benefits: it can teach teamwork, build confidence, and increase academic success. Students who take regular physical education classes not only develop healthier habits throughout their lives, but the activity reduces anxiety and improves judgment. One student revealed that students who did not have access to these classes were 2.5 times more likely to become inactive. Some students may feel awkward in physical education class; however, they may be getting more out if it than they realize.

Write at least one sentence at the beginning of the paragraph that establishes a clear claim. Type your answer in the space provided.

What is required for a student to do well on this question? Certainly, the ability to put together a strong sentence (or sentences) is needed, but in this case, composing the sentence requires some complex thinking—the sentence has to be comprehensive, coherent, and persuasive. The sentence has to be comprehensive in that it encompasses the details of the whole sentence. It has to be coherent in that it logically and skillfully prepares the reader for what comes next. Finally, it has to be persuasive because the claim must be one that the reader is prepared to accept after reading the rest of the paragraph.

Given the complexity of the task, it is only fair that students have opportunities to understand this kind of task and also practice responding to it. How can we provide these opportunities without succumbing to merely "teaching to the test"? Some creativity is called for. This task is not a natural part of the writing process. Usually a writer knows very well what his or her claim is before composing material to support that claim. However, there may be opportunities to practice this skill in an authentic writing situation by specifically asking students to find and evaluate the claim for another student's piece of writing.

Here is an example. Marica, an 18-year-old English language learner, has written a response to the following prompt:

Write an essay giving your opinion on the following statement: The young can learn a lot about life from old people.

The young can learn a lot about life from older people.

When people are getting older, some people start to be sad, miserable and angry, but not my grandfather. He is very old and he barely walks. He always has some good story to share with you. Long ago, he got a military suit, which is for his funeral. He put it in a closet. Everything was fine until one day, he decided to open his closet, but inside he couldn't find his suit. We thought that he would be sad and miserable. Instead, he made a joke. He said: "I got a suit for a funeral, but the suit has magically disappeared, so I can not die now." His story tells me about a way of looking at life. That it is not everything so sad and miserable, that you should continue with your life even in the hardest of times.

Marica has a great story illustrating what young people can learn from older people, but she needs a claim that answers the prompt. Marica could exchange papers with a peer who could help her by suggesting some possible sentences. In this way, the peer (and Marica, who would be doing the same activity) gains practice at composing a topic sentence that establishes a claim, and Marica gains feedback on her essay that can help her in revising.

Another way to provide authentic practice with this skill is through reading. Writing about what one is reading helps develop active reading skills. This can be done in any subject area. Students can be asked to write a topic sentence for this paragraph. Doing so helps the student to read more actively and transform what she or he has just read, which aids comprehension.

Math example: Here is a passage from an online open reference textbook on geometry.

Student directions: Write a topic sentence for the following paragraph:

Two line segments are congruent if they have the same length. But they need not lie at the same angle or position on the plane. Two angles are congruent if they have the same measure. So if two separate angles have measures of 30° and 23°, for example, they are not congruent because they have different measures. Congruent angles may lie in different orientations or positions. Two circles are congruent if they have the same size. The size can be measured as the radius, diameter, or circumference. They can overlap. Congruent polygons have an equal number of sides, and all the corresponding sides and angles are congruent. However, they can be in a different location, rotated, or flipped over.

(Page, John. Math Open Reference Project. July 5, 2013.
http://www.mathopenref.com/congruent.htm)

On the website, the paragraph is preceded by the following topic sentence:

Two objects are congruent if they have the same dimensions and shape. Very loosely, you can think of it as meaning 'equal', but it has a very precise meaning that you should understand completely, especially for complex shapes such as polygons.

Writing the topic sentence not only helps students understand congruency better, but they also gain practice at a skill they will need for this kind of question on the CCSS assessment.

Sentences That Refer to Sources

Many students have difficulty incorporating source texts into their writing, and it is an essential skill for college students as well as for many careers. The capacity to incorporate sources effectively requires that students gain facility in writing different kinds of sentences, so students need practice with composing these kinds of sentences.

Rookies tend to compose a sentence that looks something like this:

Author + the verb *said* + quotation:
For example: Steven Sheinkin said, "Oppenheimer complained that Secretary of State Byrnes didn't seem to understand the implications of the bomb" (215–216).

There is nothing wrong with this sentence. It makes correct attribution to the author for the quoted material and includes a parenthetical citation. However, when students are relying heavily on material from source texts during a writing-on-demand assessment, this construction will soon become repetitive. Continuing repetition of *said* does not enhance the quality of sentences. The following list provides alternatives students can use with quotes:

- suggest
- state
- contend
- note
- exclaim
- assert
- elaborate
- shout

- detail

- explain

Now that we have some stronger verbs, students can experiment with those, as well as modify the basic formula above to fit with their own prose. For example:

Quotation + the verb + author:

"Oppenheimer complained that Secretary of State Byrnes didn't seem to understand the implications of the bomb," stated Sheinkin (215–216).

Online 9.14
*Models for In-
Text Citations*

Quotation + verb & author + more quotation:

"Oppenheimer complained," suggested Sheinken, "that Secretary of State Byrnes didn't seem to understand the implications of the bomb" (215–216).

Notes on College Readiness

If we consult the "Framework for Success in Postsecondary Writing," we don't find any explicit mention of sentences. However, one could surmise that sentence sense is presumed under writing processes and knowledge of conventions—two of the writing experiences listed in the document. College writers are expected to have a strong enough grasp of the skills of writing to be able to make choices about what kinds of sentences will be most effective in a particular rhetorical context. In their careers, writers are expected to be able to write correctly and work within the conventions of their field. Teachers can foster this readiness by providing students opportunities to examine the craft of writing in a variety of fields. Some of the activities we have described in this chapter, such as sentence analysis and imitation, can be combined with an exploration of writing craft in different fields. For example, in science class, students could be given an excerpt from scientific writing like that below and asked to analyze the sentences. What types are most prevalent? Is active or passive voice used? This kind of activity can be done most effectively prior to students' writing up their own lab reports, because then they would have an authentic writing situation in which to practice the elements of craft they have just identified.

Concluding Thoughts

As we finish preparing our manuscript for publication, we know that there will be further changes and updates in the PARCC and SBAC assessments by the time the book lands in your hands. Change has always been a constant for teachers, but these days the rate of change has sped up, requiring all of us to reboot, redesign, rearrange, and rethink what we do. Sometimes it feels as if we are flying a plane while still building it.

One thing is for certain: we need to collaborate. We can't do it alone. We have to work with our colleagues—be they down the hall, at the next building, in higher education, across the country, or in one of our professional organizations. There is support available in consulting each other, strength in consensus-building around new curricula, and power in collective action. It is a time to tap into those rhetorical skills we teach our students each day and use them to shape the future for our students.

These students will face a complex world of communication, filled with rhetorical situations that are varied, challenging, and always changing. The assessments associated with the Common Core State Standards offer one challenge, but it is only one in the variety of contexts, audiences, and purposes students will contend with when they write—in college, in the working world, and in their personal lives—to give voice to their knowledge and views, and to make a difference.

References

Aldred, Jessica, Amanda Astell, Rafael Behr, Lauren Cochrane, John Hind, Anna Pickard, Laura Potter, Alice Wignall, and Eva Wiseman. 2008. "The World's 50 Most Powerful Blogs." *The Guardian*. March 9. Retrieved 9/19/2013 from www.theguardian.com/technology/2008/mar/09/blogs.

Baldwin, James. 1933. "Stranger in the Village." In *Ways of Reading*, eds. David Bartholomae and Anthony Petrosky (93–102). New York: Bedford/St. Martins.

Bunn, Mike. 2011. "How to Read Like a Writer." *Writing Spaces*. Retrieved 9/20/2013 from http://writingspaces.org/bunn--how-to-read-like-a-writer.

Carson, Rachel. 2002. *Silent Spring*. Boston: Houghton Mifflin.

Christenbury, Leila. 2000. *Making the Journey: Being and Becoming a Teacher*. 2nd ed. Portsmouth, NH: Heinemann.

Christensen, Francis. 1963. "A Generative Rhetoric of the Sentence." *College Composition and Communication* 14 (3): 155–161.

Clark, Irene. 2012. "Students' Awareness of Genre and Rhetoric." Paper read at National Council of Teachers of English Conference, November 16. Las Vegas, NV.

College Entrance Examination Board. 2003. "The Neglected 'R': The Need for a Writing Revolution." New York: The National Commission on Writing in America's Schools and Colleges. Retrieved 9/20/2013 from www.writingcommission.org/prod_downloads/writingcom/neglectedr.pdf.

Common Core State Standards Initiative. 2010. "Common Core State Standards for English Language Arts & Literacy in History/Social Studies, Science, and Technical Subjects. Appendix A: Research Supporting Key Elements of the Standards, Glossary of Key Terms." ERIC. Retrieved 9/20/2013 from www.eric.ed.gov/?id=ED522007.

Council of Writing Program Administrators, National Council of Teachers of English, and National Writing Project. 2011. "Framework for Success in Postsecondary Writing." Retrieved 9/20/2013 from http://wpacouncil.org/framework.

Daniels, Harvey, Steven Zemelman, and Nancy Steineke. 2007. *Content-Area Writing*. Portsmouth, NH: Heinemann.

Daviss, Bennett and Marlene Thier. 2002. *New Science Literacy: Using Language Skills to Help Students Learn Science*. Portsmouth, NH: Heinemann.

Dickens, Charles. (1859) 1998. *A Tale of Two Cities*. New York: Dover.

Didion, Joan. 1980. "Good-bye to All That." In *Slouching Toward Bethlehem*. San Francisco: Farrar, Straus, and Giroux.

Douglass, Frederick. 1845. *Narrative of the Life of Frederick Douglass, an American Slave. Written by Himself.* Boston: Anti-Slavery Office. Retrieved 8/19/2013 from http://www2.hn.psu.edu/faculty/jmanis/f-douglas/narrative-douglass.pdf.

Dunsmore, Kailonnie. 2012. "Creating a Culture of Teacher Learning: Thinking about the Common Core Standards Systemically." July 18. *National Center for Literacy Education.* Retrieved 9/20/2013 from www.literacyinlearningexchange.org/blog/creating-culture-teacher-learning-thinking-about-common-core-standards-systemically.

Elbow, Peter. 1981. *Writing with Power: Techniques for Mastering the Writing Process.* New York: Oxford University Press.

Flocabulary. 2013. "Metaphors and Similes in Hip-Hop." Retrieved 9/20/2013 from www.flocabulary.com/hiphopmetaphors/.

Gallagher, Kelly. 2006. *Teaching Adolescent Writers.* Portland, ME: Stenhouse.

Gere, Anne, Leila Christenbury, and Kelly Sassi. 2006. *A Student Guide to Writing on Demand: Strategies for High-Scoring Essays.* Portsmouth, NH: Heinemann.

———. 2005. *Writing on Demand: Best Practices and Strategies for Success.* Portsmouth, NH: Heinemann.

Graham, Steve, and Delores Perin. 2007. "Writing Next: Effective Strategies to Improve Writing of Adolescents in Middle and High School." A Report to Carnegie Corporation of New York. Washington, DC: Alliance for Excellence in Education, 2007.

Heller, Rafael, and Cynthia L. Greenleaf. 2007. "Literacy Instruction in the Content Areas: Getting to the Core of Middle and High School Improvement." Alliance for Excellent Education. Retrieved 9/20/2013 from www.all4ed.org.

Joos, Martin. 1967. *The Five Clocks: A Linguistic Excursion into the Five Styles of English Usage.* New York: Harcourt.

Kittle, Penny. 2008. *Write Beside Them.* Portsmouth, NH: Heinemann.

Krathwohl, David R. 2002. "A Revision of Bloom's Taxonomy: An Overview." *Theory into Practice* 41 (4): 212–218.

Maxwell, Rhoda. 1995. *Writing Across the Curriculum in Middle and High Schools.* Des Moines, IA: Allyn & Bacon.

National Council for Teachers of English. 2012. "NCTE/IRA Standards for the English Language Arts." Retrieved 9/20/2013 from www.ncte.org/standards/ncte-ira.

———. 1985. "Resolution on Curriculum Development." Retrieved 9/20/2013 from www.ncte.org/positions/statements/currdevelopment.

NCTE Executive Committee. 2013. "NCTE Position Statement on Machine Scoring. Retrieved 9/20/2013 from www.ncte.org/positions/statements/machine_scoring.

NCTE James R. Squire Office of Policy Research. 2012. "Reading Instruction for *All* Students." A Research Policy Brief of the National Council of Teachers of English."

Retrieved 9/19/2013 from www.ncte.org/library/NCTEFiles/Resources/Journals/
CC/0221-sep2012/Chron0221PolicyBrief.pdf.

———. 2012. "Using Evidence in Writing." Policy Brief. Retrieved 9/20/2013 from www.
ncte.org/library/NCTEFiles/Resources/Journals/CC/0222-nov2012/CC0222Policy.
pdf.

National Public Radio. 2013. "This I Believe." Retrieved 9/20/2013 from www.npr.org/
series/4538138/this-i-believe.

National Writing Project. Retrieved 9/20/2013 from www.nwp.org/.

New York State Education Department. *Engage NY*. 2012. "Common Core Shifts."
Retrieved 9/20/2013 from www.engageny.org/resource/common-core-shifts.

O'Brien, Peggy. 2006. *Shakespeare Set Free: Teaching Romeo and Juliet, Macbeth and
Midsummer Night's Dream*. New York: Simon and Schuster.

Ovid. *Metamorphoses: Daedalus and Icarus*. Retrieved 11/29/2013 from http://hompi.
sogang.ac.kr/anthony/Classics/OvidIcarus.htm.

Page, John. 2013. *Math Open Reference Project*. 5 July. Retrieved 9/20/2013 from www.
mathopenref.com/congruent.html.

Partnership for Assessment of Readiness for Colleges and Careers. 2013. "Grade
11—ELA/Literacy." Retrieved 9/20/2013 from www.parcconline.org/samples/
english-language-artsliteracy/grade-11-elaliteracy.

Partnership for Assessment of Readiness for College and Careers (PARCC). 2012. "Task
Prototypes and Sample Items." PARCC Online. Retrieved 9/20/2013 from www.
parcconline.org/samples/item-task-prototypes.

———. 2012. "Grade 7 Prose Constructed Response from Research Simulation Task." Retrieved
9/20/2013 from www.parcconline.org/samples/english-language-artsliteracy/grade-7-
prose-constructed-response-research-simulation-task.

———. 2012. "Grade 10 ELA/Literacy." Retrieved 9/20/2013 from www.parcconline.org/
samples/english-language-artsliteracy/grade-10-elaliteracy.

Reiss, Gertrude, 1997. "Naftale." In *The Perceptive I: A Personal Reader and Writer*, eds.
Edmund J. Farrell and James E. Miller, Jr. (49–53). Lincolnwood, IL: NTC.

Segalove, Ilene and Paul Bob Velick. 1996. *List Yourself: Listmaking as a Way to Self Discovery*. Kansas City, MO: Andrews McNeel.

Sexton, Anne. 1999. "To a Friend Whose Work Has Come to Triumph." *The Complete
Poems*. New York: Houghton Mifflin Harcourt.

Sheinkin, Steve. 2012. *Bomb: The Race to Build—and Steal—the World's Most Dangerous
Weapon*. New York: Roaring Brook Press.

Smarter Balanced Assessment Consortium. May 29, 2013. "Practice Test." Retrieved
9/20/2013 from www.smarterbalanced.org/pilot-test/.

———. 2013. "8th Grade ELA." Retrieved 9/20/2013 from http://dese.mo.gov/divimprove/assess/documents/asmt-sbac-ela-gr8-sample-items.pdf.

———. 2012. "Grade 11 Performance Task." Retrieved 9/20/2013 from www.smarterbalanced.org/wordpress/wp-content/uploads/2012/09/performance-tasks/nuclear.pdf.

Storybird. 2013. Retrieved 9/20/2013 from http://storybird.com/.

Stryker, William G. 1970. "Review of *Transformational Sentence-Combining, a Method for Enhancing the Development of Syntactic Fluency in English Composition* by John C. Mellon." *The English Journal* 59 (6): 862–865.

Taylor, Mildred. 2004. *Roll of Thunder, Hear My Cry*. New York: Puffin.

———. 2001. *The Land*. New York: Speak.

Toplak, M. E., C. Dockstader, and R. Tannock. 2006. Traitement de l'information temporelle dans leTDAH: les résultats à ce jour et de nouvelles méthodes. *Journal of Neurosciences Methods* 151: 15–29.

Ujifusa, Andrew. August 19, 2013. "N.Y. Test-Score Plunge Adds Fuel to Common-Core Debate." *Education Week*. Retrieved 9/20/2013 from www.edweek.org/ew/articles/2013/08/21/01newyork.h33.html?tkn=ZRNFFA6AHcgo6CmqxF%2BY2k AajDBJTx5OslWD&cmp=ENL-EU-NEWS2.

Viegas, Jennifer. 2012. "Dinosaurs on the Road to Extinction Before Asteroid Strike." Retrieved 9/20/2013 from http://news.discovery.com/animals/dinosaurs/dinosaurs-extinction-asteroid-120501.htm.

Wiggins, Grant, and Jay McTighe. 2005. *Understanding by Design*. Alexandria, VA: Association for Supervision and Curriculum Development.

Index